Christmas Made Easy

Recipes, Tips & Edible Gifts for a Stress-Free Holiday

By Art Ginsburg
Mr. Food

Cogin, Inc.
1770 NW 64th Street, Suite 500
Fort Lauderdale, Florida 33309

Mr. Food, OOH IT'S SO GOOD!!, the trademarks and logos and the Mr. Food likeness are registered marks owned by Ginsburg Enterprises Incorporated. All rights reserved.

Our thanks to the following companies for providing products for our food photography:

The Homer Laughlin China Company, makers of Fiesta® Dinnerware

250°C plus POLETTO, makers of porcelain kitchenware from ASA SELECTION

Temp-tations®
Temp-tations® is a Registered Trademark of Coastal Sales Associates, Inc., all rights reserved. Old World©, Old World Rustico© and Sonoma are registered Temp-tations® copyrighted designs of Coastal Sales Associates, Inc., all rights reserved.

Library of Congress Cataloging-in-Publication Data

Ginsburg, Art.
        Mr. Food Christmas Made Easy: recipes, tips and edible gifts for a stress-free holiday / by Art Ginsburg.

ISBN 978-0-9755396-0-6

1. Cookery. 2. Christmas. I. Title: Mr. Food Christmas Made Easy. II. Title.

Printed in the United States of America

First Edition

www.MrFood.com

Introduction

The holidays are...

supposed to be the most wonderful time of the year! So why are most of us so stressed? Maybe it's 'cause we dream of a white Christmas, imagining that we're gonna get everything decorated, wrapped, and cooked to perfection as if we have elves hidden away somewhere! Nice dream. The reality? This is the most hectic time of year for most of us! We're running in every direction, our homes may look like a storm blew through, and we could use help putting the "festive" back into the festivities!

That's what inspired me to write *Mr. Food Christmas Made Easy*. I'm dedicating this book to everyone who wants to bring back the magic of the season. It's chock-full of recipes that look as good as they taste. And the best part? They're a cinch to throw together!

Now that you've got this book in your hand, I can't wait for you to begin turning the pages because what's waiting for you are over 150 awesome recipes that'll have you covered whether you're throwing a bash, need something special to take along to a get-together, or want to create edible gifts for family and friends. No worries – it's all at your fingertips!

And I'm betting that this cookbook will not only get you through the hectic holiday season, but it will be perfect for entertaining throughout the year! Think of it as a bonus gift...from me to you.

So, what are you waiting for? Your "elves" have arrived...and they're hiding in every page! This will be your go-to holiday cookbook year after year 'cause, you know me, I've packed it with lots of..."OOH IT'S SO GOOD!!®"

Art Ginsburg
(or, as you know me, "Mr. Food")

Acknowledgments

We all know it would be impossible for Santa...

to deliver all those gifts without the help of his elves, reindeer and, of course, Mrs. Claus, right? Of course, right! And, just like Santa, besides having a beard, a belly laugh, and absolutely loving food, I, too, have an incredible team of people behind me. They've helped me make this Christmas cookbook really special for you.

First I want to thank Howard Rosenthal for sharing his creative vision, and for challenging our entire team to make this book truly spectacular. Howard, who wears many hats, and I have worked side by side for over 16 years and, along the way, we've had lots of fun tasting recipes in our test kitchen, as well as recreating them on my TV set. I thank you, Howard.

Speaking of my test kitchen, there's nobody I'd rather have heading it up than Patty Rosenthal. For countless cookbooks and thousands of TV segments, Patty has been the person who always made sure every recipe turned out "just so," while adhering to my quick & easy, tasty philosophy. For this book in particular, Patty shared many of her family favorites, so you're in for a real treat! I also want to tip my chef's hat to Jaime Gross, who added a lot of skill and a little magic to every recipe as she diligently tested and retested each one.

I want to thank my editor, my daughter Caryl Ginsburg Fantel, who once again helped me craft my every word and made sure each recipe is as easy to follow as it is yummy. Thank you, Caryl, for your constant attention to detail.

Two veterans on our editorial team, Helayne Rosenblum and Jodi Flayman, certainly helped make this book come together by adding lots of ho-ho-ho to every page and organization to the entire project...you gals are incredible! And for really bringing everything to life, I want to thank Erica DiMaio, who took all the recipes and photos and magically designed and transformed them into a true keepsake of a cookbook.

And if you find yourself drooling over the photos, credit needs to go to Hal Silverman Studios. Hal and his production assistant Frank Schram are truly amazing, and a pleasure to work with! I also want to thank Rachel Johnson for capturing the how-to photos, making many of the recipes even easier to follow. What a team!

For making sure everything always runs smoothly, I want to thank my son Steve Ginsburg who heads up the administrative side of our business, and Lina Nin and Carol Ginsburg for their finance and administrative support. And, of course, where would I be without my own "Mrs. Claus"...my wife Ethel, who keeps me happy, looking good, and always in the right place at the right time.

I also want to thank all the people and companies who, in one way or other, helped create such a fun and tasty cookbook. You know who you are...and you know how much I appreciate all you do.

But the most important thanks go to you, my viewers and readers, who have shared so much of yourselves with my team and me over the years, and who make everything we do so rewarding. We thank you all and wish you a very Merry Christmas!

Contents

Introduction...iii

Acknowledgments...............................iv

Notes...vi

Christmas Breakfast..............................1

Appetizers & Munchies.......................17

Soups & Salads.....................................37

The Bread Basket.................................51

Entertaining Entrées............................61

Festive Go-Alongs...............................83

Survival Meals.....................................101

Sweet Endings.....................................113

Cookies, Bars & More........................137

Santa's Sippers....................................163

Gifts from the Kitchen........................171

Index..185

Notes

Christmas Breakfast

Strawberry Breakfast Rollups....................2

Bananas Foster Waffles..............................4

Chocolate-Stuffed French Toast...............5

Broccoli and Cheese Quiche......................6

Overnight Strata...7

Cheddar 'n' Egg Pinwheels........................8

Stuffed Pancake Muffins..........................10

Country Ham & Potato Hash...................11

Tiramisù Pancakes....................................12

Cranberry Citrus Muffins........................13

Very Cherry Coffee Cake.........................14

Cinnamon Breakfast Wreath...................16

Strawberry Breakfast Rollups

Makes 2 dozen

*T*here's nothing more fun or festive for breakfast than these strawberry rollups. You can make 'em up in advance then bake 'em up warm and golden for all Santa's little (and big) helpers.

1 (8-ounce) package cream cheese, softened

2 tablespoons strawberry jelly

1 egg yolk

1 cup sugar, divided

24 slices white sandwich bread, crusts removed

1 tablespoon ground cinnamon

3 tablespoons butter, melted

Sliced strawberries and blueberries for topping, optional

1 In a medium bowl, beat cream cheese, strawberry jelly, egg yolk, and 1/4 cup sugar until smooth; set aside.

2 Roll out each bread slice with a rolling pin. Spread cheese mixture over bread, distributing evenly. Roll up each slice jellyroll-style and place seam-side down on a baking sheet.

3 In a shallow dish, combine remaining 3/4 cup sugar and the cinnamon. Brush melted butter over rollups then roll them in the cinnamon-sugar mixture, until completely coated. Repeat with remaining rollups, placing them on baking sheet after coating.

4 Cover and freeze at least 2 hours, or up to 2 months.

5 Just before serving, preheat oven to 400°F. Bake rollups 10 to 12 minutes, or until golden. Serve as is or topped with berries.

MAKE-AHEAD TIP: These are perfect for making in advance and having on hand to bake up fresh when you want them, both at the holidays and throughout the year.

Bananas Foster Waffles

Serves 4

*B*ananas Foster is a decadent dessert that was born in New Orleans. On Christmas (or any other day you choose), everybody deserves to feel special, so indulge in that same rich Louisiana taste tradition. Get your day started off on a sweet note.

8 frozen waffles

6 tablespoons (3/4 stick) butter

3/4 cup packed brown sugar

1/8 teaspoon ground cinnamon

4 large bananas, peeled and sliced

1 Preheat oven to 425°F.

2 Place waffles on a rimmed baking sheet and heat 6 to 7 minutes, or until hot.

3 Meanwhile, in a large skillet, melt butter over medium heat. Add brown sugar and cinnamon; stir until sugar is melted. Stir in bananas, cook 1 to 2 minutes, or until heated through.

4 Spoon banana mixture over waffles and serve immediately.

GARNISHING TIP: To give this just the right finishing touch, top with whipped cream and a sprinkle of cinnamon.

Chocolate-Stuffed French Toast

Serves 6

Who knew French toast could be so chocolaty?! If Old Saint Nick knew you were serving this, he and his reindeer surely would have stuck around for breakfast!

1 (1-pound) loaf day-old French bread

1 cup (6 ounces) milk chocolate chips

5 eggs

1-1/4 cups milk

1/4 teaspoon ground cinnamon

1/4 teaspoon vanilla extract

1 Coat a 9" x 13" baking dish with nonstick cooking spray. Slice bread into 1-1/2-inch slices. Using a small serrated knife, cut a 2-inch-long slit horizontally in one side of each bread slice, cutting 3/4 of the way through, creating a pocket in each.

2 Spoon 2 heaping teaspoons chocolate chips into the pocket of each bread slice; press to close. Place filled slices in baking dish.

3 In a medium bowl, whisk together eggs, milk, cinnamon, and vanilla. Pour mixture evenly over bread, turning pieces over to coat completely. Cover with plastic wrap and refrigerate several hours or overnight.

4 Preheat oven to 400°F. Bake stuffed bread, uncovered, for 20 to 25 minutes, or until golden.

SERVING TIP: Give this the perfect finishing touch by drizzling with chocolate syrup.

Broccoli and Cheese Quiche

Serves 6 to 8

Quiche works for any get-together, at any time of day! This light yet flavor-packed dish cooks up for a colorful Christmas breakfast or party hors d'oeuvre.

1 cup (4 ounces) shredded yellow Cheddar cheese

1 cup (4 ounces) shredded Swiss cheese

1 (10-ounce) package frozen chopped broccoli, thawed and well drained

1 frozen ready-to-bake 9-inch pie shell, thawed

2 eggs

1 cup half-and-half

1 teaspoon onion powder

1/4 teaspoon black pepper

1/4 teaspoon ground nutmeg

1 Preheat oven to 350°F.

2 In a medium bowl, combine Cheddar cheese, Swiss cheese, and broccoli; mix well then sprinkle into pie shell.

3 In a small bowl, beat eggs, half-and-half, onion powder, and pepper until thoroughly combined. Pour into pie shell; sprinkle with nutmeg.

4 Bake 40 to 45 minutes, or until firm and a wooden toothpick inserted in center comes out clean. Cool 5 minutes then slice and serve.

MAKE-AHEAD TIP: Make this a day or two before you plan to serve it. Cover and store it in the fridge then slice when cold. You can reheat all of it in the oven or just a piece or two in the microwave when you want it.

Overnight Strata

Serves 8

*T*his is the perfect dish for Christmas morning 'cause you can put it together in advance and pop it in the oven while everybody's opening their presents. When they're done, so is the strata!

16 (1/2-inch) slices egg bread *or* white bread

3 cups (12 ounces) shredded Swiss cheese, divided

8 eggs

2-1/2 cups milk

1 teaspoon mustard powder

2 teaspoons onion powder

1/2 teaspoon salt

1/2 teaspoon pepper

1 Coat a 9" x 13" glass baking dish with nonstick cooking spray. Place 8 slices of bread on bottom of dish then sprinkle with 1-1/2 cups cheese. Place remaining bread slices over cheese then sprinkle with remaining cheese.

2 In a medium bowl, whisk together remaining ingredients. Pour over bread and cheese, cover, and refrigerate 2 hours or overnight.

3 Preheat oven to 350°F. and bake 50 to 60 minutes, or until puffy and golden, and the center is set.

MAKE-AHEAD TIP: If you're assembling this in advance, be sure not to bake it until just before serving. This is a dish you want to serve right out of the oven.

Cheddar 'n' Egg Pinwheels

Serves 4 to 6

*L*ooking for a new way to serve eggs on a busy morning? If so, mark this page, 'cause you'll be making this recipe a lot. These eggs are festive-looking with plenty of cheesy flavor in every bite!

6 eggs

1-1/2 cups milk

1/2 cup all-purpose flour

1/2 teaspoon salt

1/2 teaspoon black pepper

5 scallions (green onions), thinly sliced, optional

1 cup (4 ounces) shredded Cheddar cheese

1 Preheat oven to 350°F. Line a 10" x 15" rimmed baking sheet with aluminum foil then coat foil with nonstick cooking spray.

2 In a large bowl, whisk together the eggs, milk, flour, salt, and pepper for 2 to 3 minutes, or until mixture is smooth. Stir in scallions, if desired, then pour mixture onto prepared baking sheet.

3 Bake 12 to 15 minutes, or until set. Sprinkle evenly with cheese then bake 2 to 3 minutes, or until cheese is melted.

4 Allow to cool 5 minutes then carefully lift aluminum foil (eggs and all) and remove from baking sheet. Starting from a smaller end, roll up eggs jellyroll style, carefully removing the aluminum foil as you roll. Slice into 1-inch pieces and serve.

Stuffed Pancake Muffins

Makes 1 dozen

*T*here's nothing like those big old-fashioned breakfasts Mom used to make with piles of pancakes and bacon or sausage. On Christmas morning, we don't have time for all that, but we can still capture those flavors with our pancake muffins.

2 cups packaged pancake and waffle mix

2 eggs

1 cup milk

1/2 cup club soda

1 tablespoon vegetable oil

4 heat-and-serve beef sausages, chopped (half of a 5.2-ounce package)

1/4 cup pancake syrup

1 Preheat oven to 350°F. Coat a 12-cup muffin tin with nonstick cooking spray.

2 In a large bowl, combine pancake mix, eggs, milk, club soda, and oil; mix well. Pour evenly into muffin cups and sprinkle each with sausage.

3 Bake 20 to 25 minutes, or until a wooden toothpick inserted in center comes out clean. Remove from oven and brush tops with pancake syrup. Serve warm.

CHANGE IT UP: Instead of sausage, these can also be made with crumbled bacon, fresh blueberries or peeled and chopped apples.

Country Ham & Potato Hash

Serves 6

What a great way to use up some of your holiday ham! I suggest making a double batch, 'cause this holds up really well for reheating.

1/2 cup (1 stick) butter

1 large onion, diced

1 (2-pound) bag frozen hash brown potato cubes, thawed

1/2 teaspoon garlic powder

1/2 teaspoon black pepper

1/2 pound (1-1/2 cups) diced cooked ham

1 In a large skillet, heat butter over high heat and sauté onions 3 to 4 minutes, until soft.

2 Add hash brown potatoes, garlic powder, and pepper, and cook 15 minutes, or until potatoes begin to brown.

3 Stir in the ham and cook 5 to 6 more minutes, or until heated through.

MAKE-AHEAD TIP: If you'd like, you can put this together in advance and simply reheat it on Christmas morning.

Tiramisù Pancakes

Serves 6

Start Christmas day with an international flair by serving these Italian-inspired pancakes after all the presents are opened.

2 (12-count) packages frozen pancakes

1 (8-ounce) package cream cheese, softened

1 (8-ounce) container mascarpone cheese

2/3 cup confectioners' sugar

1 teaspoon instant coffee granules

2 tablespoons water

1 tablespoon unsweetened cocoa

1 Warm pancakes according to package directions.

2 Meanwhile, in a large bowl, beat cream cheese, mascarpone cheese, and confectioners' sugar until well combined.

3 In a small bowl, dissolve coffee granules in water then add to cheese mixture; mix well.

4 Place a pancake on a plate then dollop with cheese mixture; repeat layers two more times, ending with a dollop of cheese mixture topping the stack.

5 Repeat with remaining pancakes and cheese mixture. Sprinkle with cocoa and serve immediately.

PREPARATION TIP: Don't need to serve 6 for breakfast? No problem. This filling will last up to a week in the fridge, or it can even be frozen and used whenever you want to take a taste trip to Europe.

Cranberry Citrus Muffins

Makes 1 dozen

*F*resh-out-of-the-oven muffins are a welcome addition to any breakfast or brunch. Slather on some butter or drizzle with a bit of honey and watch 'em disappear.

1 cup chopped fresh *or* frozen cranberries

3/4 cup plus 3 tablespoons sugar, divided

2 cups all-purpose flour

2 teaspoons baking powder

1/2 teaspoon salt

1/2 cup (1 stick) butter, softened

3/4 cup orange juice

1 egg

1/2 cup sour cream

1 Preheat oven to 375°F. Coat a 12-cup muffin tin with nonstick cooking spray (see note).

2 In a small bowl, combine cranberries and 2 tablespoons sugar; toss gently and set aside.

3 In a large bowl, combine flour, 3/4 cup sugar, the baking powder, and salt; mix well. Stir in butter until mixture is crumbly.

4 Stir in orange juice, egg, and sour cream; mix well. Gently stir in cranberry mixture then spoon batter equally into muffin cups and sprinkle tops with remaining 1 tablespoon sugar.

5 Bake 25 to 30 minutes, or until a wooden toothpick inserted in center comes out clean. Allow to cool 10 minutes then remove from pan. Serve warm, or allow to cool before serving.

CHANGE IT UP: If you prefer, use holiday-themed paper or foil muffin tin liners.

Very Cherry Coffee Cake

Serves 15

*Y*um! What smells and tastes better than a fresh-baked coffee cake? I can't think of anything...and neither will you after you experience this one bursting with plump, ruby red cherries.

1 cup (2 sticks) butter

1-1/2 cups sugar

3 eggs

3 cups all-purpose flour

2 teaspoons baking powder

1 teaspoon vanilla extract

1 (21-ounce) can cherry pie filling

Topping:

1/4 cup all-purpose flour

1/4 cup sugar

2 teaspoons butter

1 teaspoon ground cinnamon

1 Preheat oven to 350°F. Coat a 9" x 13" baking pan with nonstick cooking spray.

2 In a large bowl, cream 1 cup butter and 1-1/2 cups sugar; add eggs, one at a time. Add 3 cups flour, the baking powder, and vanilla; mix well.

3 Spread half the batter into prepared pan; spread cherry pie filling evenly over batter and, using a wet knife, cover evenly with remaining batter.

4 In a small bowl, using a fork, mix together topping ingredients until crumbly. Sprinkle over batter.

5 Bake 55 to 60 minutes, or until a wooden toothpick inserted in center comes out clean. Cool in pan on a wire cooling rack. Cut and serve.

Cinnamon Breakfast Wreath

Serves 6

*T*he first time I made this, I almost ate the whole cake by myself...well, I wanted to, but I didn't, and I don't recommend trying that. Instead, I do recommend sharing it with family and friends, or they might not share any presents with you under the tree!

1 (17.3-ounce) can refrigerated buttermilk biscuits (8 biscuits)

1 (10.8-ounce) can refrigerator buttermilk biscuits (5 biscuits)

1 tablespoon butter, melted

1/2 cup granulated sugar

2 teaspoons ground cinnamon

1/2 cup raisins

1/2 cup chopped walnuts

1/2 cup confectioners' sugar

4 teaspoons milk

1 Preheat oven to 350°F. Coat a 10-inch Bundt pan with nonstick cooking spray.

2 Separate the large can of biscuit dough into 8 biscuits and the small can into 5 biscuits. Cut each biscuit into 6 pieces and place pieces in a large bowl. Pour melted butter over biscuit pieces.

3 In a small bowl, combine granulated sugar, cinnamon, raisins, and nuts. Sprinkle sugar mixture over biscuit pieces and toss until well coated then place dough into prepared Bundt pan, distributing evenly.

4 Bake 25 minutes, or until center is firm. Let cool 10 to 15 minutes then invert Bundt pan over a plate to release the ring.

5 Before serving, in a small bowl, combine confectioners' sugar and milk to make a glaze; drizzle over ring. Serve warm.

SERVING TIP: The best way to serve this is to get right in there and pull it apart with your hands. Not only is it tasty, but it's fun to eat!

Appetizers & Munchies

Festive Stromboli..................................18

Kris Kringle Dip...................................20

Layered Buffalo Dip..............................21

Stuffed Pizza Bites................................22

Swiss Fondue Bread..............................23

Frosty the Cheese Ball..........................24

Yuletide Buttermilk Dip........................26

Dogs & Hogs......................................27

Cranberry-Pecan Brie............................28

Wicked Raspberry Wings.......................29

Easy Clams Casino...............................30

Saucy Cola Meatballs............................32

Golden Potato Puffs.............................33

Bite-Sized Crab Cakes..........................34

    Mustard Dipping Sauce.....................34

Bacon-Stuffed Deviled Eggs..................36

Festive Stromboli

Serves 8

We all need to have a secret weapon ready to go in case we get a call that friends are gonna stop by. At my house, it's this easy-to-make stromboli, and is it ever incredible!

Nonstick cooking spray

1 (13.8-ounce) can refrigerated pizza crust

8 slices Genoa *or* hard salami

6 slices deli-style ham

8 slices mozzarella cheese

1/2 cup roasted red peppers, drained and cut into strips

1 tablespoon Parmesan cheese

1/2 teaspoon garlic powder

1/8 teaspoon salt

1/8 teaspoon black pepper

1 teaspoon Italian seasoning

1 Preheat oven to 425°F. Coat a baking sheet with nonstick cooking spray.

2 Unroll pizza dough onto a flat surface. Layer with salami, ham, mozzarella cheese and roasted red pepper strips. Sprinkle with Parmesan, garlic powder, salt, and black pepper.

3 Starting with the end of the dough, roll up jellyroll-style and place on prepared baking sheet. Lightly spray stromboli with nonstick cooking spray then sprinkle with Italian seasoning.

4 Bake 15 to 18 minutes, or until golden. Let cool 5 minutes then slice and serve with your favorite marinara sauce.

Kris Kringle Dip

Serves 6 to 8

*T*his fresher, lighter version of traditional spinach and artichoke dip goes together in no time in a skillet. With this on your party table, a special guest will surely stop by to taste the dish named in his honor. Kris Kringle won't be able to resist it...and neither will your guests!

1 tablespoon butter

1 (8-ounce) package low-fat cream cheese

1 garlic clove, chopped

1 (6-ounce) package baby spinach

1 (14-ounce) can artichoke hearts, drained and chopped

1/2 cup light sour cream

1/2 cup shredded part-skim mozzarella cheese

1/2 teaspoon salt

1/8 teaspoon ground red pepper

2 tablespoons diced pimiento, drained

1 In a large skillet, melt butter over medium-high heat. Add cream cheese and garlic; cook 3 to 4 minutes, until cream cheese melts, stirring constantly.

2 Stir in spinach and cook until wilted. Stir in remaining ingredients and cook until cheese is melted and mixture is heated through. Serve immediately.

MAKE-AHEAD TIP: Simply store this in a microwave-safe dish and, just before serving, reheat in the microwave until smooth and creamy, stirring occasionally.

Layered Buffalo Dip

Serves 6 to 8

*E*verybody knows Buffalo is famous for its chicken wings. I should say it's famous for its lip-smackin' good, messy chicken wings. Here's a way to enjoy that great Buffalo wing flavor but without the messy fingers or the chicken bones!

1 (8-ounce) package cream cheese, softened

1-1/2 cups diced, cooked chicken

2 stalks celery, chopped

1/3 cup Buffalo wing hot sauce

1 cup blue cheese dressing

1 cup shredded mozzarella cheese

1 Preheat oven to 350°F. Spread cream cheese evenly over bottom of a 9" pie plate.

2 In a medium bowl, combine chicken, celery and hot sauce. Mix well then spoon over cream cheese. Pour blue cheese dressing over chicken then sprinkle top with mozzarella cheese.

3 Bake 15 to 18 minutes, or until heated through and cheese is melted.

SERVING TIP: Serve this with nacho chips and go all the way with celery sticks, too, for the true Buffalo wing experience.

Stuffed Pizza Bites

Makes 10

I'm gonna give you a heads-up: Before you start this recipe, plan on making a double batch, 'cause everyone loves these. And you'd better plan on giving your friends their own copies of this book, too, 'cause, after they taste these, they'll definitely ask you to share the recipe.

1 (7.5-ounce) can refrigerated biscuits (10 biscuits)

Dried oregano for sprinkling

Garlic powder for sprinkling

10 (1-inch) cubes mozzarella cheese (5 ounces total)

2 tablespoons spaghetti sauce

1 Preheat oven to 375°F. Lightly coat a baking sheet with nonstick cooking spray.

2 Separate biscuit dough into 10 pieces. Make an indentation in the center of each piece with your thumb. Lightly sprinkle each indentation with oregano and garlic powder; top each with a cheese cube.

3 Pull dough over cheese and pinch dough together firmly to completely enclose the cheese. (It's important to close these totally, to prevent the cheese from oozing out during baking.) Place seam-side down 2 inches apart on prepared baking sheet.

4 Lightly brush tops with spaghetti sauce then refrigerate for 15 minutes.

5 Bake 10 to 12 minutes, until golden. Serve warm.

MAKE-AHEAD TIP: You can prepare these in advance, keep them in the fridge, then bake 'em right before serving.

Swiss Fondue Bread

Makes about 20 slices

*E*verybody loves the taste of cheese fondue, but nobody likes the work and cleanup of making it the traditional way. Now you can have the Old World taste but "today entertaining easy"!

1/3 cup mayonnaise

1/4 cup dry white wine

2 tablespoons sliced scallions
  (green onions)

2 tablespoons Dijon mustard

2 cups shredded Swiss cheese

1 (1-pound) loaf French bread,
  cut into 1/2" rounds

1 Preheat oven to broil.

2 In a medium bowl, combine mayonnaise, wine, scallions, and mustard; mix well then stir in Swiss cheese.

3 Place bread rounds on a rimmed baking sheet and toast under broiler 2 to 4 minutes, or until lightly browned. Remove from oven and cool slightly before spreading the cheese mixture evenly on each.

4 Just before serving, broil until cheese is golden and bubbly.

SERVING TIP: I like to serve these rounds topped with a drizzle of raspberry sauce that I make by melting some raspberry jelly in the microwave for a few seconds.

Frosty the Cheese Ball

Serves 10 to 12

Why serve plain old cheese and crackers when we can have a super-looking centerpiece that doubles as a tasty snowman cheese ball on the table? This is an old favorite, but it's so popular that I had to bring it back again – and now it's even a little lighter.

2 (8-ounce) packages reduced-fat cream cheese, softened

1 (3-ounce) container real bacon bits

1-1/4 cups finely chopped walnuts

1/4 cup light mayonnaise

2 scallions (green onions), finely chopped

1/2 cup chopped fresh parsley

1 tablespoon horseradish

1/4 teaspoon crushed red pepper

1 In a large bowl, combine all ingredients; mix well.

2 Divide mixture into 3 balls: 1 small, 1 medium, and 1 large.

3 Arrange balls on a serving platter to form a snowman lying down. Garnish as desired (see Tip) then serve, or cover and chill until ready to serve.

GARNISHING TIP: It's fun to garnish this with black olives for the eyes and mouth, a baby carrot for the nose, and red pepper pieces for buttons, but feel free to use any of your favorite edible delights. Don't forget the crackers!

Yuletide Buttermilk Dip

Makes about 1-1/2 cups

You can't have a holiday party without a veggie dip, so keep this recipe on hand for a lighter version that's always inviting. That's right, by using buttermilk, it's actually lower in fat and calories than it would be with low-fat milk!

1 cup light mayonnaise

1/2 cup buttermilk

1/4 cup sun-dried tomatoes

1/2 teaspoon garlic powder

1/4 teaspoon mustard powder

1/4 teaspoon salt

1/4 teaspoon black pepper

1 In a blender or food processor, blend all ingredients on medium speed until smooth.

2 Cover and chill until ready to serve.

MAKE IT HOLIDAY-FESTIVE: Go ahead and sprinkle on chopped parsley to give this a really festive look.

Dogs & Hogs

Serves 8

For all the bacon-lovers among us, this is the appetizer you've been waiting for: hot dogs wrapped in bacon with a cherry-honey-mustard dipping sauce. You're gonna be in hog heaven!

cup yellow mustard

/2 cup maraschino cherries

tablespoons honey

tablespoon cherry juice

2 slices bacon, cut in half (24 pieces)

hot dogs (about 1 pound), cut into thirds (24 pieces)

1 Preheat oven to 400°F. In a blender or food processor, combine mustard, cherries, honey, and cherry juice; process until smooth.

2 Meanwhile, wrap bacon around hot dog pieces, and place on baking sheet. Bake 8 minutes, turning hot dogs over, and cook 5 to 6 more minutes, or until bacon is crisp.

3 Serve with cherry-honey-mustard dipping sauce.

Cranberry-Pecan Brie

Serves 6

*T*his savory and sweet snack is a hit at the holidays and all throughout the year. Make this easy, tasty hors d'oeuvre for your next get-together. Enjoy the raves!

1 (8-ounce) container refrigerated crescent dinner rolls

1 (8-ounce) round Brie cheese

3 tablespoons whole-berry cranberry sauce

3 tablespoons chopped pecans, divided

1 egg, beaten

1 Preheat oven to 350°F. Coat a rimmed baking sheet with nonstick cooking spray.

2 Unroll crescent dough and press dough at perforations to seal. Slice Brie in half horizontally and place bottom half in center of dough.

3 Spread cranberry sauce over top, sprinkle with 2 tablespoons pecans and replace top of Brie. Bring dough up over top of Brie, pressing dough firmly to seal. Place seam-side down on baking sheet; brush with beaten egg and sprinkle with remaining pecans.

4 Bake 25 to 30 minutes, or until deep golden. Let cool 5 to 10 minutes before serving. Using a serrated knife, cut into wedges.

SERVING TIP: I suggest serving this with a bowl of warmed whole-berry cranberry sauce so guests can spoon it over each slice for an even fruitier flavor.

Wicked Raspberry Wings

Serves 4

Y ou want to serve wings for your holiday get-together, but you don't want to be seen as a "me-too" host. Try these and you'll hear "Fruity!" "Crispy!" and "Just the right kick!" after each bite. Oh, I almost forgot: You'll hear "Incredible!" too!

1/3 cup soy sauce

1 tablespoon chopped fresh garlic

1/2 teaspoon black pepper

1 (5-pound) bag split chicken wings and drumettes, thawed if frozen

1/2 cup seedless raspberry jam

1/4 cup sweet chili sauce

1 In a large bowl or baking dish, combine soy sauce, garlic, and pepper. Add chicken wings then toss to coat well. Cover and marinate in the refrigerator for 1 hour.

2 Preheat oven to 400°F. Line two large rimmed baking sheets with aluminum foil and coat foil with nonstick cooking spray.

3 Remove chicken from marinade and discard marinade. Spread wings in a single layer on prepared baking sheets.

4 Bake wings 55 to 60 minutes, or until no pink remains and wings are crispy.

5 Meanwhile, in a medium bowl, combine jam and chili sauce; mix well. Transfer wings to a large bowl and pour glaze over them. Toss wings to coat completely then serve immediately.

Easy Clams Casino

Makes 1 dozen

I've made preparing traditional Clams Casino easier than ever. Instead of shucking the raw clams, we steam them first, so they open by themselves! Yup, this is a simple shortcut for restaurant-style Clams Casino that the whole gang will enjoy, including the chef du jour.

12 large clams, scrubbed

1 (4-ounce) can mushroom stems and pieces, drained

3/4 cup Italian-flavored bread crumbs

1/2 medium-sized red bell pepper, coarsely chopped

1/2 medium-sized red onion, coarsely chopped

3 slices bacon

1 Preheat oven to 400°F. Fill a large soup pot with 1 inch of water and add the clams. Cover and bring to a boil over high heat; cook 3 to 5 minutes, or until clams open. Pull off and discard top shell of each clam.

2 Meanwhile, in a food processor, combine remaining ingredients and process until smooth. Spoon bread crumb mixture over clams and place on a baking sheet. Bake 25 to 30 minutes, or until lightly browned on top and heated through. Serve immediately.

SERVING TIP: To really make this a show-stopper, line an **ovenproof** 9" x 13" platter with kosher salt. Heat it in the oven for a few minutes to get the salt hot. Nestle the cooked clam shells in the hot salt. They'll look great and the hot salt will help keep the clams warm!

Saucy Cola Meatballs

Makes about 4 dozen

*H*ave you ever noticed where everybody gathers at a party? Around the meatballs! They won't be able to get enough of these babies, so be sure to make plenty! *Check 'em out in the photo one page back.*

1 pound ground beef

1 cup seasoned bread crumbs

2 tablespoons water

1 small onion, finely chopped, divided

1 teaspoon salt, divided

1/2 teaspoon black pepper, divided

1 garlic clove, minced

1 cup ketchup

1 cup cola

1 tablespoon Worcestershire sauce

1 Preheat oven to 325°F.

2 In a large bowl, combine ground beef, bread crumbs, water, half of the onion, 1/2 teaspoon salt, and 1/4 teaspoon black pepper; mix well. Form into 1-inch meatballs and place in a 9" x 13" baking dish.

3 In a medium bowl, combine remaining ingredients, including remaining onion, 1/2 teaspoon salt, and 1/4 teaspoon black pepper; mix well.

4 Pour mixture over meatballs and bake 50 to 60 minutes, or until meatballs are cooked through and sauce is bubbling.

Golden Potato Puffs

Makes about 72 small puffs

*T*hese little puffs are amazing because they get brushed with egg yolk before baking, and that creates a crust that everybody loves.

3 pounds potatoes, peeled
   and quartered (see Tip)

1 large onion, chopped

3 tablespoons olive oil

1 cup cracker crumbs

2 teaspoons salt

1/2 teaspoon black pepper

2 egg yolks, beaten

1 Preheat oven to 400°F.

2 Place potatoes in a soup pot and add just enough water to cover them. Bring to a boil over high heat then reduce heat to medium and cook 12 to 15 minutes, or until fork-tender. Drain off water, mash potatoes, and allow to cool slightly.

3 Coat a baking sheet with nonstick cooking spray. In a small saucepan, heat oil over medium heat then sauté onion until tender. Add sautéed onion, the cracker crumbs, salt, and pepper to mashed potatoes; mix well.

4 With your hands, roll mixture into 1-inch balls and place potato balls on prepared baking sheet. Brush with egg yolk.

5 Bake 40 to 45 minutes, or until golden and crusty.

PREPARATION TIP:
These work best if you use Idaho potatoes because they have just the right moisture content and hold up the best.

Bite-Sized Crab Cakes

Makes 2 dozen

*I*t's the holidays, which means it's time to pull out all the stops! Well, these crab cakes are the real deal, whether you make 'em cocktail-sized for an hors d'oeuvre or bigger for a main dish.

1 egg

1 tablespoon mayonnaise

1 teaspoon Dijon mustard

1 teaspoon seafood seasoning
(like Old Bay)

8 saltine crackers, finely crushed

1 pound jumbo lump crabmeat
(see Find It)

1 Preheat oven to 350°F. Coat a baking sheet with nonstick cooking spray.

2 In a large bowl, lightly beat the egg. Add mayonnaise, mustard, seafood seasoning, and crushed crackers; mix well.

3 Gently stir in crabmeat until thoroughly combined. Shape mixture by tablespoonfuls into 24 patties and place on prepared baking sheet.

4 Bake 12 to 15 minutes, or until lightly browned. Serve as is or with Mustard Dipping Sauce.

FIND IT: You can usually find fresh jumbo lump crabmeat at your local supermarket seafood counter, or canned in the refrigerated or freezer section of your market.

Mustard Dipping Sauce

1 tablespoon plus 1/2 teaspoon
mustard powder

1 cup mayonnaise

2 teaspoons Worcestershire sauce

1 teaspoon steak sauce

2 tablespoons heavy cream

2 tablespoons milk

Salt to taste

1 In a small bowl, whisk together mustard powder and mayonnaise. Beat in remaining ingredients until blended and creamy. Serve chilled.

Bacon-Stuffed Deviled Eggs

Makes 2 dozen

*E*verybody loves deviled eggs, so why not give 'em the unexpected? This version featuring bacon and Cheddar cheese is guaranteed to liven up your party!

12 hard-cooked eggs, peeled

1/2 cup mayonnaise

1/4 cup sour cream

1-1/2 teaspoons Dijon mustard

1 teaspoon lemon juice

1/4 cup bacon bits

1/4 cup finely shredded sharp
   Cheddar cheese

2 tablespoons chopped fresh chives
   or scallions (green onions)

1/8 teaspoon black pepper

1 Cut eggs in half lengthwise. Scoop yolks into a medium bowl; set aside egg white halves.

2 Add remaining ingredients to egg yolks; mix well.

3 Fill egg white halves with yolk mixture (see Tip) and place on a platter. If desired, garnish with additional bacon bits and finely shredded Cheddar cheese. Cover with plastic wrap and refrigerate until ready to serve.

TEST KITCHEN TIP: Place egg mixture in a resealable plastic storage bag, seal, and cut tip off one corner of bag (make sure it's big enough to allow bacon and scallions through). Pipe egg mixture into egg white halves.

Soups & Salads

Escarole and Meatball Soup....................38

Creamy Mushroom Soup.......................40

Harvest Pumpkin Soup..........................41

Velvety Corn Soup.................................42

Busy-Night Soup...................................43

Ultimate Caesar Salad...........................44

    Parmesan-Garlic Croutons....................44

Black Forest Salad.................................45

Reindeer Crunch Salad..........................46

Raspberry Vinaigrette............................46

Greek Isles Salad..................................48

Pear-Walnut Spinach Salad....................49

Honey-Mustard Dressing........................50

Farmer's Dressing.................................50

Escarole and Meatball Soup

Serves 6 to 8

When it comes to the holidays, each nationality has its own traditions. Every year, some good friends of mine make this soup that originated with their Italian heritage. Trust me, it's irresistible, no matter what culture you come from!

1/2 pound ground beef

1/4 cup Italian-flavored bread crumbs

1/4 cup water

3/4 teaspoon black pepper, divided

8 cups chicken broth

1/2 cup chopped fresh escarole *or* spinach

2 medium carrots, finely chopped

1/2 cup tiny shell pasta

1/4 cup grated Parmesan cheese

1 In a medium bowl, combine the ground beef, bread crumbs, water, and 1/4 teaspoon pepper; mix well then form into 1/2-inch meatballs.

2 In a soup pot, combine the chicken broth, escarole, carrots, meatballs, and remaining 1/2 teaspoon pepper. Cover and bring to a boil over high heat. Reduce the heat to low and simmer, covered, for 30 minutes.

3 Add pasta (see Tip), increase heat to medium, and cook 8 to 10 minutes, or until pasta is tender. Sprinkle with Parmesan cheese, and serve.

TEST-KITCHEN TIP: If you're making this in advance, add the pasta while reheating so it doesn't absorb all the broth.

Creamy Mushroom Soup

Serves 8 to 10

*T*hick and creamy, and studded with loads of mushrooms, this soup is so good that you'd better start off with extra-big bowls!

1/4 cup (1/2 stick) butter

2 pounds fresh mushrooms, sliced (see note)

1-1/2 teaspoons onion powder

1/2 teaspoon black pepper

1 cup all-purpose flour

7 cups beef *or* chicken broth

2 cups half-and-half

1 In a soup pot, melt butter over medium heat. Add mushrooms, onion powder, and pepper; sauté 5 to 6 minutes, or until mushrooms are tender.

2 Stir in flour for about 1 minute, or until absorbed. Slowly stir in broth and bring to a boil.

3 Reduce heat to medium-low, add half-and-half, and simmer 25 to 30 minutes, or until slightly thickened, stirring occasionally.

4 Cover, remove from heat, and let sit for 10 minutes to thicken before serving.

CHANGE IT UP: Our markets have quite a variety of mushrooms available throughout the year, so go ahead and experiment with different ones.

Harvest Pumpkin Soup

Serves 5 to 7

Sure, we usually think of pumpkins at Halloween and Thanksgiving, but why not try this soup with your Christmas dinner? It's a super way to start off this festive meal.

1 (29-ounce) can pure pumpkin

1-3/4 cups chicken broth

1/2 cup water

1/4 cup packed light brown sugar

1/2 teaspoon ground nutmeg

1/2 teaspoon salt

1/8 teaspoon black pepper

2 cups half-and-half

1 In a large saucepan, combine all ingredients except half-and-half; mix well. Bring to a boil over medium heat, stirring frequently.

2 Reduce heat to low and stir in half-and-half until well blended. Cover and simmer until heated through. Serve immediately.

SERVING TIP: Make this extra festive by topping each bowl with a dollop of sour cream before serving. For a really spectacular presentation, serve soup in individual hollowed-out small pumpkins.

Velvety Corn Soup

Serves 4 to 6

Nothing is more comforting than a steamin' hot bowl of soup to say "Welcome home." So, at the holidays, if you find yourself looking for just the right easy meal or meal starter, I suggest this is the way to go.

3-1/2 cups chicken broth

2 (14-3/4-ounce) cans creamed corn

1/4 teaspoon black pepper

1 tablespoon water

2 teaspoons cornstarch

1 egg, beaten

2 scallions (green onions),
   thinly sliced

1 In a large saucepan, combine chicken broth, creamed corn, and pepper; bring to a boil over medium-high heat.

2 In a small bowl, combine water and cornstarch until smooth. Add to broth mixture and simmer 2 to 3 minutes, or until slightly thickened, stirring occasionally.

3 Swirl beaten egg slowly into soup, forming thin strands. Top with sliced scallions right before serving.

MAKE-AHEAD TIP: Yes, it's okay to make the soup in advance and simply reheat it when ready to serve.

Busy-Night Soup

Serves 8 to 10

Whether you're hustling about to get your shopping done or scrambling to put the finishing touches on the tree, this soup is just what you need. It serves a bunch and is just as good the next day...maybe even better.

2 tablespoons olive oil

2 medium-sized onions, chopped

5 garlic cloves, minced

5-1/4 cups chicken broth

2 (20-ounce) cans cannellini beans, undrained

1 (14-1/2-ounce) can diced tomatoes, undrained

1/2 teaspoon salt

1 teaspoon black pepper

1 cup uncooked ditalini *or* other small shaped pasta

1/2 cup chopped fresh parsley

1 In a large soup pot, heat oil over medium heat; sauté onions and garlic about 10 minutes, or until onions are tender.

2 Stir in chicken broth, 1 can of cannellini beans, the tomatoes, salt, and pepper; cook 30 minutes, stirring occasionally.

3 Meanwhile, cook pasta according to package directions then drain.

4 Using a potato masher, gently mash beans and tomatoes in soup pot. Add remaining can of beans, the parsley, and the cooked pasta. Reduce heat to low and simmer 30 minutes, stirring occasionally.

SERVING TIP: Give this a finishing touch (for both looks and taste!) by topping each serving with a bit of fresh grated Parmesan cheese.

Ultimate Caesar Salad

Serves 4 to 6

*I*f you're a Caesar salad-lover like I am, get ready for a real treat. This salad is so good that maybe, just maybe, you might think of putting a plate of salad out for Santa instead of cookies.

2 (10-ounce) bags romaine lettuce, washed

1 cup mayonnaise

1/2 cup milk

2 tablespoons fresh lemon juice

1/2 cup plus 1 tablespoon grated Parmesan cheese, divided

2 garlic cloves, minced

1/2 teaspoon salt

1/2 teaspoon black pepper

1 (2-ounce) can anchovies in oil, drained (optional)

Parmesan-Garlic Croutons (see below)

1 Place romaine in a large bowl; set aside.

2 In a medium bowl, combine mayonnaise, milk, lemon juice, 1/2 cup Parmesan cheese, the garlic, salt, and pepper; whisk until smooth and creamy.

3 Add dressing to romaine; toss to coat well.

4 Top with anchovies, if desired, and sprinkle with the remaining 1 tablespoon Parmesan cheese. Serve immediately as is or topped with Parmesan-Garlic Croutons (below).

Parmesan-Garlic Croutons

2 cups cubed leftover bread

2 tablespoons olive oil

1/2 teaspoon garlic powder

1 tablespoon Parmesan cheese

1/8 teaspoon salt

1/8 teaspoon black pepper

1 Preheat oven to 375°F.

2 In a medium bowl, combine bread, oil, garlic powder, Parmesan cheese, salt, and pepper; toss until evenly coated.

3 Place bread mixture evenly on a rimmed baking sheet and bake 15 to 20 minutes, or until golden.

44

Black Forest Salad

Serves 4 to 6

I love how the unique flavors of this salad marry so well and complement main dishes like roast turkey and glazed ham...and so will you!

2 tablespoons peanut oil

1/4 cup coarsely chopped pecans

1/3 cup honey

1/4 cup maple syrup

1/2 cup Italian dressing

1 (10-ounce) bag romaine lettuce, washed

1 (14-ounce) can dark pitted cherries, drained

1 In a medium saucepan, combine oil and pecans; heat over medium heat until nuts are golden, stirring frequently.

2 Add honey, maple syrup and dressing; reduce heat to low, and simmer 5 to 7 minutes, or until heated through.

3 Meanwhile, place lettuce on a large salad platter and top with cherries. Pour hot dressing over salad, toss gently, and serve immediately.

Reindeer Crunch Salad

Serves 5

*J*ust wait 'til you bring this change-of-pace salad to the holiday table this year. It's loaded with crunch and goodness that'll make everyone happy, especially the reindeer.

1 (5-ounce) bag mixed baby greens

1/2 cup dried cranberries

1/2 cup roasted pumpkin seeds

1/4 cup diced red onion

1/2 cup crumbled goat cheese (optional)

Raspberry Vinaigrette (see below)

1 In a large salad bowl, combine the greens, cranberries, pumpkin seeds, red onion, and goat cheese, if desired. Prepare Raspberry Vinaigrette then, just before serving, drizzle 1/4 cup dressing over salad and toss until evenly coated, adding more as desired.

Raspberry Vinaigrette

Makes 1-1/4 cups

1/2 cup seedless raspberry jam *or* preserves

2 tablespoons balsamic vinegar

2 tablespoons Dijon mustard

1/4 teaspoon black pepper

1/4 cup olive oil

2 tablespoons water

1 In a medium bowl, whisk together the jam, vinegar, mustard, and pepper until thoroughly combined. Whisk in oil then water. Add to salad as directed above; cover and refrigerate any remaining dressing.

Greek Isles Salad

Serves 4 to 6

I've heard that Christmas in Greece is absolutely amazing. Unfortunately, it's not something that many of us will have a chance to experience firsthand. Instead, bring the tastes of the Greek islands right to your table.

3/4 cup olive oil

1/3 cup fresh lemon juice

1 tablespoon dried oregano

1/2 teaspoon garlic powder

1/2 teaspoon salt

1/4 teaspoon black pepper

1 medium head iceberg lettuce, cut into 1-inch chunks

1 medium cucumber, peeled and diced

1 (4-ounce) package crumbled feta cheese

2 medium tomatoes, cut into wedges

1 (6-ounce) can pitted large black olives *or* Greek olives, drained

1 In a small bowl, combine oil, lemon juice, oregano, garlic powder, salt, and pepper; mix well.

2 Place chopped lettuce on a platter. Top with cucumber then sprinkle with feta cheese. Arrange tomatoes over cheese then top salad with olives. Drizzle dressing over salad and serve.

FIND IT: Greek olives can be found at most supermarket deli counters or in the ethnic foods section.

Pear-Walnut Spinach Salad

Serves 5

*F*ruit and cheese on a salad go hand in hand like a Christmas tree and twinkling lights or wrapping paper and tape. That's why I think this recipe is worth adding to your list of holiday must-haves.

/2 cup olive oil

3 tablespoons white vinegar

/4 cup sugar

/2 teaspoon celery seeds

/4 teaspoon salt

(10-ounce) package fresh spinach, washed and trimmed

-1/2 cups walnut halves, toasted

ripe red pears, cored and sliced

ounces crumbled blue cheese

1 In a small bowl, combine oil, vinegar, sugar, celery seeds, and salt; mix well.

2 In a salad bowl, combine remaining ingredients. Add dressing mixture; toss gently until well combined. Serve immediately.

Honey-Mustard Dressing

Makes about 2 cups

*E*ven though this recipe is in the salad chapter, don't be shy about slathering it on your leftover ham or turkey. It's the best honey-mustard dressing I ever tasted... and I'm a homemade dressing fanatic!

1-1/4 cups mayonnaise

1/3 cup honey

2/3 cup vegetable oil

1 tablespoon white vinegar

1 teaspoon minced onion flakes

2 tablespoons chopped fresh parsley

2 tablespoons yellow mustard

1 In a medium bowl, whisk together all ingredients until smooth and creamy.

2 Serve immediately, or cover and chill until ready to use.

Farmer's Dressing

Makes about 2 cups

I got this light, creamy dressing from a farmer during the cucumber harvest a few years back, and am I glad I did! Now I get to enjoy this fresh-from-the-garden taste all year long...and so can you!

1 medium cucumber *or* zucchini, cut into small chunks

1 cup sour cream

1 cup mayonnaise

1/2 teaspoon garlic powder

1/4 teaspoon black pepper

1 In a food processor or blender, blend all ingredients on medium-high speed until smooth. Serve immediately, or cover and chill until ready to serve.

The Bread Basket

Sour Cream & Chive Biscuits..................52

Chive Butter..52

Olive Focaccia...54

Kickin' Corn Bread..................................55

Honey Butter..55

Easy Mayo Rolls.....................................56

Candy Cane Bread Sticks......................57

Bacon Cheddar Rollups.........................58

Pumpkin Spice Bread............................60

Sour Cream & Chive Biscuits

Makes about 1 dozen

Move over, ordinary biscuits! These fresh 'n' flaky homemade biscuits will run rings around store-bought! The flavorful sour cream and chive twist makes them a holiday stand-out.

2-1/2 cups biscuit baking mix

1 tablespoon chopped fresh chives

1 cup sour cream

Flour for dusting

1 Preheat oven to 450°F. Coat a rimmed baking sheet with nonstick cooking spray.

2 In a large bowl, combine baking mix and chives; mix well. Add sour cream, and knead 2 to 3 minutes, or until dough forms a soft ball.

3 Place on a lightly floured surface and use a rolling pin to roll out to 1/2-inch thickness. With a 3-inch biscuit cutter, cut dough into biscuits and place on prepared baking sheet.

4 Bake 15 to 18 minutes, or until light golden. Serve plain or with Chive Butter (below).

Chive Butter

1/2 cup (1 stick) butter, softened

1 tablespoon chopped fresh chives

1 In a small bowl, combine butter and chives. Serve immediately, or cover and chill until ready to use. Let soften at room temperature for 15 to 20 minutes before serving.

Olive Focaccia

Makes 12 to 16 pieces

Whether your gang is naughty or nice, they're gonna appreciate the homemade goodness of this easy Italian-style bread studded with olives. *Check out the photo one page back to see how tempting it looks.* No need to let 'em in on your secret shortcut: frozen bread dough!

1 pound frozen bread dough, thawed

1 teaspoon olive oil

1/2 cup pitted chopped kalamata *or* other ripe black olives (see note)

1/2 cup pitted chopped Sicilian *or* other green olives (see note)

2 tablespoons shredded Parmesan cheese

1/2 teaspoon dried oregano

1 Preheat oven to 450°F. Coat a 10" x 15" baking sheet with nonstick cooking spray.

2 Using your fingertips or the heel of your hand, spread dough to cover bottom of pan. Push dough up to edge of pan, forming a rim. If dough is too sticky, dust it and your hands lightly with flour. With a fork, prick dough 15 to 20 times. Brush dough with oil. Sprinkle evenly with olives then top with cheese and oregano.

3 Bake 12 to 15 minutes, or until focaccia is crisp and brown. Cut in half then cut each half into 6 to 8 strips for easy serving.

FIND IT: Kalamata and Sicilian olives can usually be found at the deli counter in larger supermarkets, and sometimes you can even find them pitted. If not, make sure to cut the olive away from the pit before placing on dough.

Kickin' Corn Bread

Makes 12 to 15 pieces

*O*ur classic homemade corn bread gets a spicy kick from zesty jalapeño peppers. Imagine teaming this one with comforting Fire Station Chili (page 112) to enjoy after a busy shopping day at the mall!

2 (8.5-ounce) packages corn muffin mix, batter prepared according to package directions

2 tablespoons vegetable oil

4 jalapeño peppers, chopped (see Tip)

1/2 cup canned *or* frozen corn kernels

1/4 cup sour cream

2 tablespoons honey

1 Preheat oven to 400°F. Coat a 9" x 13" baking dish with nonstick cooking spray.

2 In a large bowl, combine corn muffin batter with remaining ingredients; mix well. Pour into prepared baking dish.

3 Bake 18 to 20 minutes, or until golden. Let cool then cut and serve as is or with Honey Butter (below).

PREPARATION TIP: When handling hot peppers, don't let the peppers come in contact with your eyes or skin. Protect yourself by wearing food-safe gloves.

Honey Butter

1/2 cup (1 stick) butter, softened

2 tablespoons honey

1 In a small bowl, combine butter and honey. Stir until smooth and creamy. Serve immediately, or cover and chill until ready to use. Let soften at room temperature for 15 to 20 minutes before serving.

Easy Mayo Rolls

Makes 1 dozen

*E*asy as 1-2-3, mayonnaise takes the place of eggs and oil in these incredibly moist rolls we can throw together at a moment's notice. That's just what we need during all the hustle and bustle of the holidays.

3 cups self-rising flour

1-1/2 cups milk

1/3 cup mayonnaise

1 Preheat oven to 425°F. Coat 12 muffin cups with nonstick cooking spray.

2 In a medium bowl, combine all ingredients; mix well then spoon equally into prepared muffin cups.

3 Bake 12 to 15 minutes, or until golden.

4 Serve warm, or allow to cool slightly then remove to a wire rack to cool completely.

TEST KITCHEN TIP: Most of us keep milk and mayonnaise on hand all the time, but you've gotta be sure to have self-rising flour on hand, too, so you can mix and bake these up any time.

Candy Cane Bread Sticks

Makes about 2 dozen

Now we can have two kinds of candy canes on the table: traditional candy ones and these bread stick ones, perfect for dunking in hearty soup or chili. Make no mistake, these are tasty enough to gobble down all by themselves...and they're festive, too.

- (10-ounce) package refrigerated pizza dough
- tablespoon butter, melted
- /4 teaspoon garlic powder
- /4 teaspoon salt
- tablespoon poppy seeds (see note)

1 Preheat oven to 425°F. Unroll pizza dough on a work surface.

2 In a small bowl, combine butter, garlic powder, and salt; mix well then brush over dough. Sprinkle evenly with poppy seeds.

3 Cut dough crosswise into 1/2-inch strips then make one cut lengthwise, cutting all strips in half. Twist each strip into a swirled pattern then form into a candy cane shape and place 1 inch apart on ungreased baking sheets.

4 Bake 5 to 7 minutes, or until golden around edges.

CHANGE IT UP: These can also be opped with dried onion flakes or any avorite seasonings.

Bacon Cheddar Rollups

Makes 8

*A*t holiday time, it's the little extra homemade efforts that really count. These easy crescent rollups are short on work and long on taste 'cause they're chock-full of a flavorful combo of ingredients.

1 (8-ounce) can refrigerated crescent dinner rolls

3 tablespoons ranch dressing

1/4 cup cooked real bacon pieces

1/2 cup finely shredded Cheddar cheese (see note)

1/4 cup chopped scallions (green onions)

1 Preheat oven to 375°F. Unroll dough and separate into 8 triangles.

2 Spread dressing to edges of each triangle Sprinkle evenly with bacon, cheese, anc scallions.

3 Starting at shortest side of triangle, roll up each piece of dough and place on an ungreased baking sheet, bending each into a crescent shape.

4 Bake 11 to 13 minutes, or until golden. Serve immediately, or remove from baking sheet to cool.

CHANGE IT UP: If you're like me and prefer your rolls really cheesy, jus sprinkle a little extra cheese over them right when they come out of the oven anc are still hot.

MEDITERRANEAN ROLLUPS: For a taste of the Mediterranean, substitute tablespoons chopped sun-dried tomatoes, 1/4 cup chopped fresh basil, and 2 tablespoons grate Parmesan cheese for the ranch dressing, bacon, Cheddar, and scallions.

SOUTH-OF-THE-BORDER ROLLUPS: Substitute 2 tablespoons tac seasoning, 1/2 cup shredded Colby-Jack cheese, and 2 tablespoons chopped fresh cilantro for th ranch dressing, bacon, Cheddar, and scallions.

Pumpkin Spice Bread

Makes 8 mini loaves

*T*hese mini bread loaves are perfect for adding to the bread basket on your holiday dinner table or for giving as a homemade gift. Either way, everybody will know they're made with love.

8 (1-pint) wide-mouthed canning jars (see Notes)

3-1/2 cups packed light brown sugar

1/2 cup (1 stick) butter, softened

1 (15-ounce) can solid-pack pumpkin

4 eggs

3-1/2 cups all-purpose flour

1-1/2 teaspoons baking powder

1 teaspoon baking soda

1 teaspoon ground cinnamon

1/2 teaspoon ground ginger

1 cup chopped pecans

1 Preheat oven to 325°F. Coat canning jars with nonstick cooking spray.

2 In a large bowl, beat brown sugar and butter 3 to 4 minutes, or until well blended. Add pumpkin and eggs, and beat 2 minutes, or until well mixed.

3 Add flour, baking powder, baking soda, cinnamon, and ginger. Beat 1 to 2 minutes, or until well blended. Stir in pecans then spoon evenly into prepared canning jars. **Do not place lids on jars.**

4 Place filled jars on a baking sheet and bake 45 to 50 minutes, or until a wooden toothpick inserted in center comes out clean. Carefully place lids on jars and seal while still hot; allow to cool completely before opening. To serve, slide bread out of jars and slice.

NOTES:

- This batter can also be baked in two 9" x 5" loaf pans (add about 20 minutes to baking time).

- The nice thing about making this in canning jars is that individual jarred loaves make great take-along gifts. Add colorful ribbon and a pretty label for the perfect way to show friends, family, co-workers, neighbors, and your kids' teachers how special they are.

- Although these are baked in canning jars, this is not a canning procedure. These can be stored 2 to 3 weeks at room temperature, or up to 2 months in the freezer.

Entertaining Entrées

Bacon-Wrapped Filets..................62
Tarragon Dijon Butter..................62
King-Cut Prime Rib..................64
Horseradish Sauce..................64
Garlic-Studded Tenderloin..................65
Mrs. Claus' Cranberry Chicken..................66
Chicken Mediterranean..................67
Honey-Dijon Ham..................68
Orchard Stuffed Pork Loin..................69
Peaches Foster Glazed Ham..................70
Herb-Crusted Pork Tenderloin..................72
Glazed Leg of Lamb..................73
Roasted Citrus Duck..................74
Pinot Grigio-Roasted Turkey..................75
Worth-the-Wait Lasagna..................76
Fresh Catch Wellington..................78
Golden-Topped Salmon..................79
Classic Lobster Thermidor..................80
Angelic Shrimp and Pasta..................82

Bacon-Wrapped Filets

Serves 4

A special occasion calls for a special main course and, with just a few ingredients, you'll have the ultimate "Wow" entrée! *The easy recipes for Jingle Bells 'n' Beans and Poinsettia Potatoes are on page 89.*

4 (5- to 6-ounce) 1-1/4-inch filet mignon steaks

1/4 teaspoon salt

1/4 teaspoon black pepper

4 slices bacon

1 Preheat broiler. Season steaks with salt and pepper.

2 In a large skillet, slightly cook bacon over medium-high heat until lightly browned but not crisp. Wrap 1 slice of bacon around each steak and secure with a wooden toothpick.

3 Place steaks on a broiler pan or rimmed baking sheet and broil 5 to 6 minutes per side for medium-rare, or until desired doneness beyond that. Remove toothpicks and serve with a scoop of Tarragon Dijon Butter (recipe below) topping each steak.

Tarragon Dijon Butter

Makes 1/2 cup

1/2 cup (1 stick) butter, softened

1 tablespoon Dijon mustard

1/2 teaspoon dried tarragon

1/8 teaspoon cracked peppercorns

1 In a medium bowl, combine butter, mustard, tarragon, and cracked peppercorns. Mix until combined then place in a crock and chill until ready to serve with steak.

King-Cut Prime Rib

Serves 6 to 8

*T*hink you need to go to a restaurant when you feel like having a nice, juicy prime rib? Uh uh! Prime rib is actually one of the easiest dishes to make. Sure, it's 'cause the oven does all the work and all we do is simply carve and enjoy.

1 (4- to 4-1/2-pound) boneless beef rib eye

1 tablespoon olive oil

1/2 teaspoon garlic powder

1/2 teaspoon onion powder

2 teaspoons salt

2 teaspoons black pepper

1 Preheat oven to 350°F. In a large roasting pan, place beef fat-side up.

2 In a small bowl, combine oil, garlic powder, onion powder, salt, and black pepper; mix well then rub over surface of beef. Roast 1-1/2 to 1-3/4 hours, or until a meat thermometer inserted in center reaches 140°F. for medium-rare, or until desired doneness beyond that.

3 Remove prime rib to a cutting board and let stand 15 to 20 minutes. Carve across the grain into thick slices and serve.

NOTE: I like to serve prime rib with this zesty Horseradish Sauce to bring out the full flavor of the meat.

Horseradish Sauce

Makes 1/2 cup

1/2 cup mayonnaise

1/3 cup prepared white horseradish, drained

1 teaspoon lemon juice

1/4 teaspoon white pepper

1 In a small bowl, combine ingredients; mix well cover, and chill at least 30 minutes before serving.

Garlic-Studded Tenderloin

Serves 10 to 12

*T*his is one of my all-time most popular fancy-schmancy meals. Not only is this simple to make, it will melt in your mouth, so get ready for lots of compliments.

1 (5- to 6-pound) whole beef
 tenderloin, trimmed

6 garlic cloves, peeled and slivered

3/4 cup soy sauce

1/4 cup olive oil

1/2 teaspoon hot pepper sauce

3/4 cup dry red wine

1 teaspoon black pepper

1 teaspoon dried thyme

1 With a paring knife, make small slits all over the tenderloin. Insert a garlic sliver into each slit; set aside.

2 In a large bowl, combine all remaining ingredients; mix well. Add tenderloin, cover and allow meat to marinate in refrigerator at least 6 hours, or overnight.

3 Preheat oven to 425°F. Remove meat from marinade and place in a roasting pan; discard marinade.

4 Roast meat 40 to 45 minutes for medium, or to desired doneness. Allow to sit 15 to 20 minutes before slicing. Slice thicker for serving as an entrée or thinner for cocktail sandwiches. Serve as is or with Horseradish Sauce (opposite page).

Mrs. Claus' Cranberry Chicken

Serves 6

*E*ver wonder what Santa does after his busy day delivering gifts all over the world? You can bet he looks forward to sitting down to Mrs. Claus' homemade Christmas dinner. Now you can serve her specialty, too!

3 cups prepared stuffing (see Note)

6 (1/2-pound) chicken breast halves, skin on and bone in (see Tip)

1 (16-ounce) can whole-berry cranberry sauce

1 tablespoon lemon juice

2 tablespoons brown sugar

1 Preheat oven to 350°F. Coat a 9" x 13" baking dish with nonstick cooking spray.

2 Stuff 1/2 cup stuffing underneath the skin of each chicken breast half. Pull skin down over stuffing to secure it in place (and keep it moist while baking). Place chicken breasts in prepared baking dish.

3 In a small bowl, combine cranberry sauce, lemon juice, and brown sugar; mix well. Spoon mixture evenly over breasts to cover.

4 Bake 55 minutes, or until juices run clear, basting occasionally.

NOTE: For the stuffing, you can use leftovers, or one 6-ounce box of stuffing mix that makes about 3 cups.

PREPARATION TIP: If you can't find chicken breasts split with the bone in and skin on, just ask the butcher to do it for you.

Chicken Mediterranean

Serves 4

With all the holiday entertaining you're planning, you'll need lots of dinner options. That's where this stuffed chicken breast fits in. I promise you rave reviews every time you serve it.

10 butter-flavored crackers

1 teaspoon butter, melted

1/4 cup sun-dried tomatoes

1/2 cup olive oil

2 tablespoons fresh parsley, stems removed

2 cloves fresh garlic, peeled

1/4 teaspoon salt

1/4 teaspoon black pepper

4 boneless, skinless chicken breasts, butterflied (see How-To)

1 (4-ounce) package goat cheese, sliced into 4 pieces

4 basil leaves

1 Preheat oven to 350°F. Coat a 9" x 13" baking dish with nonstick cooking spray. Then, in a resealable plastic storage bag, crush crackers; add butter, mix, and set aside.

2 In a blender or food processor, combine sun-dried tomatoes, oil, parsley, garlic, 1/4 teaspoon salt, and 1/4 teaspoon pepper; process until tomatoes are finely chopped.

3 Place chicken breasts on a flat surface; open them up like a book then lightly sprinkle both sides with additional salt and pepper. Place one piece of goat cheese on one half of each chicken breast and top each with a basil leaf. Evenly spoon one tablespoon of the sun-dried tomato mixture over each basil leaf.

4 Fold over top half of each chicken breast; carefully place stuffed breasts in baking dish. Spoon remaining sun-dried tomato mixture evenly over chicken and sprinkle with cracker topping. Bake 25 to 30 minutes, or until chicken is cooked through and no pink remains.

HOW-TO: To butterfly a chicken breast, place it on a flat board and place hand on top. Using a sharp knife, carefully cut horizontally three-fourths of the way through the chicken breast, so it opens like a book.

Honey-Dijon Ham

Serves 10 to 12

*T*his earned high marks in our test kitchen for both simplicity and taste. You can vary the mustard to give it a spicy or mellow taste. The choice is yours.

1 (6- to 7-pound) fully cooked ham

1/2 cup honey

1/4 cup Dijon mustard

1/2 teaspoon salt

1 Preheat oven to 325°F. Coat a roasting pan with nonstick cooking spray.

2 Place ham in prepared roasting pan and bake 1 hour.

3 In a small bowl, combine remaining ingredients; mix well. Remove ham from oven and pour glaze over entire ham.

4 Bake ham 25 to 30 more minutes. Slice and serve with pan drippings.

PREPARATION TIP: This is a cinch to put together with a fully cooked ham and just 3 other ingredients. And, while it's baking, you'll have plenty of time to get everything else ready.

Orchard Stuffed Pork Loin

Serves 6

Make this the centerpiece of your holiday table this year. Present the pork loin surrounded with greens and apple slices, and it just might be the most photographed "present" on Christmas Day!

1 (2-1/2-pound) pork loin

1/4 teaspoon salt

1/4 teaspoon black pepper

1 (6-ounce) package stuffing mix

1 cup chopped canned apples in water, drained

1 cup shredded Cheddar cheese

2 tablespoons sugar

1/2 teaspoon ground cinnamon

1/2 cup apple jelly, melted and divided

1 Preheat oven to 350°F.

2 Place pork in a large baking dish and, with a sharp knife, make a slit running lengthwise halfway down the pork *(see photo)*. Lightly sprinkle all sides with salt and pepper; set aside.

3 Prepare stuffing mix according to package directions. In a medium bowl, combine apples, cheese, sugar, and cinnamon; mix well. Gently stir apple mixture into stuffing. Spoon stuffing into slit in pork, packing it gently, and place remaining stuffing around the pork roast.

4 Cover with foil and cook 30 minutes. Remove foil and brush pork with 2 tablespoons melted apple jelly. Cook 30 more minutes then brush with another 2 tablespoons melted apple jelly.

5 Bake 5 to 10 more minutes, or until internal temperature reaches 160°F. Let sit 5 minutes then slice and serve with remaining 1/4 cup melted apple jelly.

Peaches Foster Glazed Ham

Serves 10 to 12

*H*ere's an easy way to take your holiday ham to new heights. If you'd like, stir a few fresh raspberries into the sauce just before serving to make it even more holiday-special.

1 (6- to 7-pound) fully cooked ham

1/4 cup (1/2 stick) butter

1 cup packed dark brown sugar

2 (16-ounce) cans sliced peaches, drained and cut into 1/2-inch chunks

1 Preheat oven to 325°F. Coat a roasting pan with nonstick cooking spray.

2 Place ham in pan and bake 1 hour.

3 In a medium skillet, melt butter and brown sugar over medium heat until well mixed and almost caramelized. Stir in peaches; mix well. Remove ham from oven and pour glaze over entire ham.

4 Bake ham 25 to 30 more minutes. Remove from pan and place on a serving platter. Carve at dinner table and serve with warm glaze from pan.

CHANGE IT UP: If you prefer your sauce to be sweet and spicy, add 1 teaspoon hot pepper sauce when you add the peaches.

Herb-Crusted Pork Tenderloin

Serves 6

*P*ork tenderloin is one of the best-kept secrets in our meat case. It's very reasonably priced and, since it's tender as can be, it's not only good for a main dish but it makes a super hors d'oeuvre sliced thinly and served on rounds of French bread.

2 pork tenderloins (about 1-1/4 pounds total)

2 tablespoons water

1 teaspoon browning and seasoning sauce

1 tablespoon chopped fresh parsley

1 teaspoon garlic powder

1/2 teaspoon rubbed sage

1/2 teaspoon salt

1/2 teaspoon black pepper

1 Preheat oven to 350°F. Place pork in a 7" x 11" baking dish.

2 In a small bowl, combine water and browning and seasoning sauce; mix well then spoon over pork.

3 In another small bowl, combine remaining ingredients; mix well then rub evenly over pork.

4 Bake, covered, for 25 to 30 minutes, or to desired doneness. Slice and serve with pan drippings.

Glazed Leg of Lamb

Serves 10 to 12

*L*amb is certainly a holiday tradition that's very welcome, since we don't serve it very often during the rest of the year. Serve it up for dinner with Sweet Onion Tart (page 90) and Christmas Peas (page 92), and it's sure to be this year's memory-maker.

1 (7- to 9-pound) leg of lamb

1 teaspoon salt

1/2 teaspoon black pepper

1/2 cup grape jelly

1/2 cup ketchup

1/2 cup dry red wine

1 teaspoon dried oregano

1 Preheat oven to 350°F. Fill a large roasting pan with 1/4 inch of water. Coat a roasting rack with nonstick cooking spray and place in the roasting pan.

2 Sprinkle lamb completely with salt and pepper; place on roasting rack and roast for 30 minutes.

3 In a small saucepan, combine remaining ingredients and heat over low heat until jelly melts, stirring occasionally. Brush lamb with mixture.

4 Roast lamb 3 to 3-1/2 hours, until a meat thermometer registers 160°F. for medium, or until desired doneness beyond that, brushing lamb every 30 minutes with some of the remaining jelly mixture.

5 Let lamb rest for 10 minutes before carving. Bring remaining sauce to a boil then serve with the lamb.

Roasted Citrus Duck

Serves 4

*M*ost people don't make duck at home because they think it's difficult to prepare. Well, this is the perfect recipe for duck that's flavor-packed and juicy, not fatty, thanks to my easy tips.

2 (3-1/2- to 4-pound) ducks, thawed if frozen, cut in half

2 tablespoons plus 1 teaspoon salt, divided

1 teaspoon black pepper

1 (18-ounce) jar orange marmalade

1 (11-ounce) can mandarin oranges, drained

1/8 teaspoon ground red pepper

1 Preheat oven to 450°F.

2 Season each duck on both sides with 1 tablespoon salt and 1/2 teaspoon black pepper. Place on racks in roasting pans and prick the skin all over with a fork (see Tip). Roast 45 minutes.

3 Meanwhile, in a medium bowl, combine marmalade, the remaining 1 teaspoon salt, the mandarin oranges, and ground red pepper; mix well.

4 Remove duck from oven and spread half of the marmalade mixture evenly over all four halves, reserving remaining mixture.

5 Reduce oven temperature to 350°F. and bake 25 to 30 minutes, or until juices run clear or a meat thermometer inserted in center registers 165°F. Serve duck topped with remaining sauce.

TEST-KITCHEN TIP: The secret to perfectly cooked duck is to prick the skin with a fork before cooking. That way, the fat drains out and you're left with a juicy and flavorful main dish.

Pinot Grigio-Roasted Turkey

Serves 8

Looking for a lighter-tasting main dish this year? You can stop looking. The grapes make this really fresh-tasting and, if you have any leftovers, you'll have great sandwiches, too.

1 (12- to 14-pound) turkey

1/2 pound red seedless grapes, stemmed and cut in half (about 1-1/2 cups), divided

1/2 teaspoon salt

1/2 teaspoon black pepper

1 (750-ml) bottle Pinot Grigio wine

1-3/4 cups chicken broth

2 tablespoons cornstarch

1 Preheat oven to 325°F. Line a roasting pan with aluminum foil and coat with nonstick cooking spray.

2 Place turkey in prepared pan then place 1 cup grape halves into neck cavity. Season turkey all over with the salt and pepper. Pour wine into pan around turkey.

3 Roast turkey 3-1/2 to 4-1/2 hours, or until no pink remains and juices run clear, basting turkey every 30 minutes with pan juices. If turkey begins to get too browned, cover loosely with aluminum foil.

4 In a medium saucepan, combine chicken broth, cornstarch, and pan drippings with fat removed; bring to a boil over medium-high heat, stirring constantly until thickened. Stir in remaining 1/2 cup grape halves and cook 1 to 2 minutes, or until heated through.

5 Carve turkey and serve with Pinot Grigio-grape sauce.

Worth-the-Wait Lasagna

Serves 6 to 8

*T*he name says it all, but I'd like to give you a suggestion: Don't pack this recipe away with your holiday decorations, 'cause it's definitely great for serving at family dinners and pot-lucks all year long.

12 lasagna noodles

1 pound hot Italian sausage, casing removed (see Tip)

4 cups (16 ounces) shredded mozzarella cheese, divided

1 (15-ounce) container ricotta cheese

1/3 cup grated Parmesan cheese

1 egg

1/2 teaspoon dried basil

1/2 teaspoon black pepper

2 (28-ounce) jars spaghetti sauce

PREPARATION TIP: For the true meat lover, add an extra 1/4 pound cooked, crumbled sausage on top with some shredded mozzarella cheese.

1 Preheat oven to 375°F. Cook and drain lasagna noodles according to package directions.

2 In a large skillet, cook sausage over medium-high heat until no pink remains, stirring to break up sausage as it cooks. Drain off excess liquid and set aside in a large bowl to cool slightly. Add 3 cups mozzarella cheese, the ricotta and Parmesan cheeses, the egg, basil, and pepper; mix well.

3 Coat a 9" x 13" baking dish with nonstick cooking spray. Spread 1 cup spaghetti sauce evenly over bottom of dish. Place 3 noodles over the sauce. Sprinkle one-third of cheese mixture over noodles. Pour 1 cup spaghetti sauce over cheese mixture. Place 3 more noodles over the top and press down lightly.

4 Repeat with 2 more layers of the cheese mixture, sauce, and noodles. Spoon remaining sauce over the top and cover tightly with aluminum foil. Bake 1 hour.

5 Remove foil and sprinkle remaining 1 cup mozzarella cheese over top; return to oven for 5 minutes, or until cheese has melted. Remove from oven and allow to sit 10 to 15 minutes before cutting and serving.

Fresh Catch Wellington

Serves 8

*T*his just might be the perfect main dish for a buffet. It's easy to make ahead, heats up well, and looks and tastes amazing.

1 pound (about 2 pieces) U.S. farm-raised catfish

1 (9-ounce) package frozen chopped spinach, thawed, drained, and squeezed dry

1-1/2 cups shredded mozzarella cheese

1 (4-ounce) jar diced red peppers, drained

2 tablespoons onion soup mix

1 (17.3-ounce) package frozen puff pastry, thawed

Nonstick cooking spray

MAKE-AHEAD TIP: This can be assembled and refrigerated up to 8 hours before baking, or frozen to bake off at another time.

1 Preheat oven to 375°F. Coat a baking sheet with nonstick cooking spray.

2 Place catfish on baking sheet and bake 15 to 20 minutes, or until it flakes easily with a fork. Let cool and break into bite-sized pieces.

3 In a large bowl, gently mix fish, spinach, cheese, red peppers, and soup mix until combined.

4 Unfold each puff pastry onto a large cutting board. Spoon half of the catfish mixture lengthwise down the center of each pastry sheet. Cut slits one inch apart lengthwise down each side of filling on both sheets of pastry. Braid dough over filling, overlapping to form "X" shapes.

5 Using 2 spatulas, carefully transfer filled pastries to baking sheet. Spray tops with nonstick cooking spray and bake at 400°F. for 25 to 30 minutes. Serve immediately.

Golden-Topped Salmon

Serves 4

I first served this at a holiday dinner for a friend who doesn't eat meat. Everyone wanted to try it, so my suggestion is to make this along with your meat entrée for a new take on surf and turf.

1/3 cup mayonnaise

1 tablespoon fresh lemon juice

1 garlic clove, minced

1 teaspoon dried dill weed (see Tip)

1/4 teaspoon salt

1/4 teaspoon black pepper

4 (6-ounce) salmon fillets

1 Preheat broiler. Coat a broiler pan or rimmed baking sheet with nonstick cooking spray.

2 In a small bowl, combine all ingredients except salmon; mix well. Spread mixture evenly over top of salmon.

3 Place salmon on prepared pan and broil 10 to 14 minutes, or until fish flakes easily with a fork. Serve immediately.

PREPARATION TIP: If you have fresh dill, it's fine to use a tablespoon of it, chopped, in place of the teaspoon of dried dill weed.

Classic Lobster Thermidor

Serves 4

When you're looking for the ultimate special dinner, this is the one. The best part? No reservations required!

4 (6-ounce) lobster tails, thawed if frozen

1/2 cup (1 stick) butter, divided

1/3 cup all-purpose flour

1-3/4 cups chicken broth

2/3 cup heavy cream

1/2 teaspoon paprika

1/4 teaspoon salt

1/2 teaspoon black pepper

2 tablespoons sherry

1/2 cup plain bread crumbs

1 Using a knife or kitchen shears, carefully cut away and remove the underside of the lobster tail shells; remove meat, reserving shells. Cut lobster meat into 1-inch chunks.

2 In a large skillet, melt 1/4 cup butter over medium heat. Stir in flour until well combined. Add chicken broth, cream, paprika, salt, and pepper; mix well. Stir in lobster meat, and cook 5 to 6 minutes, or until sauce is thickened and lobster turns opaque. Remove from heat and stir in sherry.

3 Preheat broiler. Place empty lobster shells on a rimmed broiler pan or baking sheet and fill with lobster mixture.

4 In a small bowl, soften remaining 1/4 cup butter and mix with bread crumbs. Sprinkle bread crumb mixture over lobster mixture and broil 2 to 3 minutes, or until golden. Serve immediately.

Angelic Shrimp and Pasta

Serves 6 to 8

*T*here is no rule book when it comes to what to serve at the holidays. That's why I suggest adding variety to your table with this Mediterranean-tasting pasta and shrimp toss. Everybody will love it.

1 (16-ounce) package
  angel hair pasta

1 pound large shrimp, peeled and
  deveined, with tails left on

2/3 cup olive oil

1/3 cup sun-dried tomatoes packed
  in oil, chopped

3 garlic cloves, crushed

2 tablespoons chopped fresh basil

1/2 teaspoon salt

1/4 teaspoon crushed red pepper

1/4 teaspoon black pepper

1/4 cup grated Parmesan cheese

1 Cook pasta according to package directions; drain, rinse, and drain again; set aside in a large bowl.

2 Meanwhile, rinse shrimp and pat dry. In a large skillet, heat oil over medium heat and add shrimp, sun-dried tomatoes, garlic, basil, salt, red pepper and black pepper. Cook 3 to 4 minutes, turning shrimp to cook evenly.

3 Add shrimp mixture to pasta then sprinkle with Parmesan cheese; toss well and serve immediately.

Festive Go-Alongs

Shredded Sweet Potato Bake..................84

Fresh Cranberry Relish.........................86

Red Pepper Pilaf...............................87

Spinach Soufflé.................................88

Jingle Bells 'n' Beans..........................89

Poinsettia Potatoes............................89

Sweet Onion Tart...............................90

Christmas Peas..................................92

Creamy Mushroom Risotto...................93

Popcorn Stuffing...............................94

Spiral Baked Potatoes.........................95

Cheddar Scalloped Potatoes..................96

Mushroom & Sausage Stuffing..............98

Southern Corn Casserole......................99

Creamy Smashed Potatoes..................100

Shredded Sweet Potato Bake

Serves 6 to 8

*T*hese don't look like the traditional sweet potatoes most of us are used to. But, boy, are they good...so good that, once you try 'em, you're gonna make 'em this way all the time!

4 sweet potatoes (about 2 pounds), peeled and shredded

1 tablespoon salt

1 cup sugar

1/2 cup light corn syrup

1/4 cup water

1/4 cup (1/2 stick) butter

1 cup pineapple juice

1 Preheat oven to 375°F. Coat a 9" x 13" baking dish with nonstick cooking spray.

2 Place potatoes in a large bowl and sprinkle with salt. Add enough ice water to just cover potatoes and let stand 10 minutes.

3 Meanwhile, in a medium saucepan, combine sugar, corn syrup, and water; bring to a boil over medium-high heat, stirring constantly. Remove from heat and stir in butter and pineapple juice until butter is melted.

4 Drain potatoes well and place in prepared baking dish. Pour sugar mixture over potatoes.

5 Bake 55 to 60 minutes, or until potatoes are tender, stirring halfway through baking.

Fresh Cranberry Relish

Makes 3 cups

'*T*is the season for magical moments and homemade yet hassle-free dishes! Although we can always take a shortcut, fresh cranberries are in season now, so it's without question the time to revel in their tangy "fresh from the bog" taste. *See how great this looks in the photo one page back.*

1 (12-ounce) package fresh or frozen cranberries

1 medium apple, unpeeled, cored and quartered

1 small seedless orange, unpeeled and quartered

1 cup sugar

1 In a food processor that has been fitted with its metal cutting blade, combine cranberries, apple, and orange. Process until finely chopped, scraping down sides of bowl as necessary.

2 Add sugar and process until thoroughly combined. Place in a medium-sized glass serving bowl, cover, and chill at least 1 hour before serving.

PREPARATION TIP: For an easy yet elegant touch, spoon relish into small glass serving dishes or martini glasses, and garnish each with an orange slice.

Red Pepper Pilaf

Serves 2 to 4

*R*ice can be dressed down for everyday, or dressed up for holidays and special dinners. This is one recipe you're gonna want in your line-up all year long. *Check it out in the photo on page 85.*

1 tablespoon butter

1 cup long- *or* whole-grain rice, divided

1 medium-sized onion, finely chopped

1-3/4 cups chicken broth

1/4 cup water

1/2 of a medium-sized red bell pepper, finely chopped

1 In a large skillet, melt butter over high heat. Add 1/2 cup rice and cook until golden, stirring constantly.

2 Add remaining rice, the onion, chicken broth, and water, and bring to a boil. Reduce heat to medium-low, cover, and simmer 15 minutes.

3 Stir in red pepper and serve.

MAKE IT HOLIDAY-FESTIVE: Chopped bell peppers and pepper strips are tops as a holiday garnish. Go even further and brighten up your holiday rice by scooping out red and green bell peppers then filling them with this pilaf to become personal-sized edible serving bowls.

Spinach Soufflé

Serves 4 to 6

Santa may tiptoe around your tree in the middle of the night, but there's no need to tiptoe around the kitchen when this rich 'n' creamy soufflé is in the oven. It's durable enough to stand up to the family and fancy enough to serve to company.

1 cup (1/2 pint) heavy cream

3 eggs

2 (10-ounce) packages frozen chopped spinach, thawed and squeezed dry

1/3 cup grated Parmesan cheese

2 tablespoons all-purpose flour

1/8 teaspoon ground nutmeg

1/8 teaspoon ground red pepper

1/2 teaspoon salt

1/4 teaspoon black pepper

1 Preheat oven to 350°F. Coat an 8-inch square baking dish with nonstick cooking spray.

2 In a medium bowl, beat heavy cream and eggs 2 to 3 minutes, or until foamy.

3 Add remaining ingredients; mix well then pour into prepared baking dish.

4 Bake 30 to 35 minutes, or until a knife inserted in center comes out clean. Cool 5 minutes before cutting into squares and serving.

Jingle Bells 'n' Beans

Serves 4 to 6

*R*ing the dinner bell to call 'em to the table for these side dishes that are sure to be the stars of your holiday table. *In case you don't believe me, check out the photo on page 63 to see their perfect holiday colors!*

1 pound fresh green beans, trimmed

1 (16-ounce) package frozen pearl onions

1/4 cup (1/2 stick) butter

1/2 teaspoon dried basil

1/2 teaspoon garlic powder

1 teaspoon salt

1/2 teaspoon black pepper

1 Place green beans in a large saucepan and add water to cover. Bring to a boil over high heat and cook 8 minutes.

2 Add onions, and cook 5 to 7 minutes, or until tender; drain and return to pot while still hot. Add remaining ingredients; mix well and serve.

Poinsettia Potatoes

Serves 4 to 6

2 quarts water

1 onion, quartered

2 teaspoons salt

2 pounds (about 20) small new red potatoes, washed

1/4 cup (1/2 stick) butter

1 garlic clove, minced

1/4 cup chopped fresh parsley

1 In a soup pot, bring water, onion, and salt to a boil over high heat.

2 Using a potato peeler, peel center one-third of each potato. Place potatoes in pot, cover, and cook 12 to 15 minutes, or just until fork-tender; drain well in a colander and keep warm.

3 Melt butter in same pot over medium heat. Add garlic, and sauté 1 to 2 minutes, or until tender. Stir in parsley then return potatoes to pot and toss to coat evenly. Serve immediately.

Sweet Onion Tart

Serves 6 to 8

*T*he only tears shed for this incredibly easy-to-make onion tart should be tears of joy over its "can't get enough of it" taste! For a novel side dish perfect for company, this one will consistently win you compliments!

1 (9-inch) frozen ready-to-bake
    pie shell, thawed

3 tablespoons butter

3 medium-sized sweet onions,
    thinly sliced

2 eggs

1 cup sour cream

1/8 teaspoon dry mustard

1/2 teaspoon salt

1/8 teaspoon black pepper

1/8 teaspoon paprika

1 Preheat oven to 350°F. Bake pie shell 8 to 10 minutes, or until light golden; set aside.

2 In a medium skillet, melt butter over high heat. Add onions, and sauté 5 minutes. Reduce heat to medium-low, cover, and sauté onions 2 to 4 more minutes, or until tender. Place sautéed onions in pie shell.

3 In a medium bowl, combine eggs, sour cream, dry mustard, salt, and pepper; mix well and pour over onions. Sprinkle top with paprika.

4 Bake 40 to 45 minutes, or until sides and crust are golden and a wooden toothpick inserted in center comes out clean. Cut into wedges and serve.

TEST-KITCHEN TIP: You're not alone! Our test-kitchen team also sheds tears when cutting onions. You see, it's a chemical reaction that occurs when the oils in the onion are released into the air. Although there are many suggested remedies, I recommend peeling the onion under cold running water. It helps.

Christmas Peas

Serves 6 to 8

No, these aren't miniature Christmas decorations. They're our version of classic peas...dressed up for the holidays. We're betting that, when you serve these, you'll be hearing "Pass the peas, please!" over and over again. *See how yummy they look on the previous page.*

1 (16-ounce) package frozen peas, thawed

1 (10-3/4-ounce) can condensed cream of mushroom soup

1 (8-ounce) can sliced water chestnuts, drained

1 (2.8-ounce) can French-fried onions, divided

1 small red bell pepper, finely chopped (see note)

1/4 cup (1/2 stick) butter, melted

1/4 teaspoon black pepper

1 Preheat oven to 350°F.

2 In a large bowl, combine all ingredients except 1 cup French-fried onions; mix well then pour into an 8-inch square baking dish and sprinkle the 1 cup reserved French-fried onions around edge.

3 Bake 25 to 30 minutes, or until heated through and bubbly.

CHANGE IT UP: The red bell pepper makes this a very colorful red and green Christmas dish, but any color bell pepper will do.

SERVING TIP: This is the time of year to break out our most festive-looking colorful baking dishes, or maybe pick up an inexpensive one at a houseware store. With sales everywhere at the holidays, imagine serving these peas from a baking dish that has some seasonal personality!

Creamy Mushroom Risotto

Serves 4 to 6

Do you need a signature side dish for the holidays? With our fool-proof tricks, creamy risotto is an Italian-style favorite that can easily become one of your specialties. So forget ordinary rice and stand out from the crowd by serving this amazing go-along!

1 cup Arborio rice

1/2 pound fresh mushrooms, sliced

1 medium-sized onion, chopped

1 teaspoon minced garlic

2 tablespoons butter, divided

3-1/2 cups chicken broth, divided

3/4 cup grated Parmesan cheese

1/8 teaspoon black pepper

1 In a large skillet, sauté rice, mushrooms, onion, and garlic in 1 tablespoon butter over medium heat, stirring constantly until onion is tender, about 5 minutes. Increase heat to high, stir in 1 cup chicken broth, and continue to cook, stirring frequently.

2 As liquid cooks down, continue to add remainder of chicken broth, 1 cup at a time. Cook for 15 to 20 minutes, until all broth is absorbed and mixture is creamy, stirring frequently.

3 Stir in Parmesan cheese, black pepper, and remaining butter. Serve immediately.

Popcorn Stuffing

Serves 6 to 8

*T*his is the ultimate in out-of-the-ordinary stuffing recipes! Who doesn't love popcorn? And as the main ingredient for dressing up a holiday bird, I'm talking about a sure holiday conversation-starter. I can't say enough great things about it, so you've just gotta try it!

6 cups crumbled corn bread *or* corn muffins (see Tips)

3 cups popped popcorn (see Tips)

1 medium-sized onion, finely chopped

1-3/4 cups chicken broth

1/2 cup (1 stick) butter, melted

2 eggs

1-1/2 teaspoons dried rubbed sage

1 Preheat oven to 375°F. Coat an 8-inch square baking dish with nonstick cooking spray.

2 In a large bowl, combine all ingredients; mix well. Spoon into prepared baking dish.

3 Bake 40 to 45 minutes, or until center is set.

TEST-KITCHEN TIPS: Ready-made corn bread or muffins can be found in the bakery section of your supermarket, or you can start from scratch and use your favorite corn bread recipe. One regular package of microwave popcorn will yield 7 to 8 cups of popcorn.

Spiral Baked Potatoes

Serves 6

Gosh, I love these — they're so simple yet so festive! Every time I serve these, I get the same questions..."Did you make these yourself?" "Are they easy?" The answer to both? YES!

6 large Idaho baking potatoes

3 tablespoons vegetable oil

1/2 teaspoon salt

1/2 teaspoon black pepper

3 (1-ounce) slices Cheddar cheese, cut in half

2 tablespoons chopped scallions *or* chives

1 Preheat oven to 400°F.

2 Place 2 wooden spoons parallel to one another on a work surface and place a potato lengthwise between the handles. Make slits three-fourths of the way through the potato, about every 1/2 inch, stopping each time the knife hits the spoon handles. Repeat with the remaining potatoes; set aside.

3 In a small bowl, combine oil, salt, and pepper; rub mixture evenly over potatoes. Place potatoes on a baking sheet and bake 55 to 60 minutes, or until tender.

4 Remove potatoes from oven and place the Cheddar cheese on top; bake 2 to 3 more minutes, until cheese is melted. Sprinkle with chopped scallions, and serve.

CHANGE IT UP: If you'd like, dollop these with sour cream and sprinkle with bacon bits to make them even more special.

Cheddar Scalloped Potatoes

Serves 6 to 8

*D*uring this hectic time of year, the taste of comfort can soothe our mall-weary souls. This creamy, homestyle potato bake will not only fit the bill for entertaining, but it's a warm and welcome addition to any dinner during the winter season.

4 cups thinly sliced white potatoes (about 6 medium potatoes)

3 tablespoons butter

2 tablespoons all-purpose flour

1-1/2 cups milk

1/2 teaspoon salt

1/2 teaspoon black pepper

1-1/2 cups shredded Cheddar cheese, divided

1 tablespoon chopped chives

1 Preheat oven to 375°F. Coat a 2-quart baking dish with nonstick cooking spray and layer with sliced potatoes.

2 In a medium saucepan, melt butter over medium heat; stir in flour until smooth. Add milk, salt and pepper; whisk until mixture begins to thicken Stir in 1 cup Cheddar cheese until melted.

3 Pour cheese mixture over potatoes then turn potatoes gently. (Try to avoid breaking them up. Cover with foil and bake 45 minutes.

4 Uncover dish then sprinkle with remaining 1/2 cup cheese and return to the oven. Bake uncovered for 10 to 15 more minutes, or until potatoes are tender. Sprinkle with chives just before serving.

CHANGE IT UP: Use different flavored shredded cheeses to give this a bit of variety each time you make it.

Mushroom & Sausage Stuffing

Serves 6 to 8

You know I always say to use any brands and adapt recipes to your family's tastes. That's what this recipe is about. We start with prepared stuffing and fancy it up with off-the-shelf ingredients. Yes, it's okay to use a shortcut or two, even on Christmas.

1 medium-sized onion, chopped

1/2 cup (1 stick) butter, melted and divided

1 (16-ounce) package ground pork sausage

1/4 pound fresh mushrooms, chopped

1-3/4 cups chicken broth

1 (8-ounce) package herb-seasoned stuffing mix

1/2 cup chopped almonds, toasted (optional)

1 egg, beaten

1 Preheat oven to 350°F.

2 In a large skillet, sauté onion in 1 tablespoon butter over medium-high heat for 5 to 7 minutes, or until golden.

3 Add sausage and mushrooms, and sauté 3 to 5 minutes, or until sausage is browned and mushrooms are tender; drain, if necessary, and set aside.

4 In a large bowl, combine chicken broth, stuffing mix, and almonds, if desired; mix well. Add remaining 7 tablespoons melted butter, the sausage mixture and egg; mix well.

5 Spoon into an 8-inch square baking dish or an 8-cup oven-proof holiday mold (see note). Cover with aluminum foil and bake 30 minutes. Uncover and bake 25 to 30 more minutes, or until heated through and top is lightly browned.

MAKE IT HOLIDAY-FESTIVE: You can bake this in any type of oven-proof shaped Christmas mold. It's nice to use a Christmas tree mold and decorate the tree with cooked frozen peas and carrots.

Southern Corn Casserole

Serves 4 to 6

*T*his southern classic comes from my good friend David, who I've worked with a lot over the years. If anyone knows good food, it's him, so I just had to share this recipe with y'all. Thanks, David!

1 (8.5-ounce) package corn muffin mix

1 (15-3/4-ounce) can whole-kernel corn, drained

1 (14-3/4-ounce) can cream-style corn

1 cup sour cream

1/2 cup (1 stick) butter, softened

1 egg

1 Preheat oven to 350°F. Coat a 2-quart casserole dish with nonstick cooking spray.

2 In a large bowl, combine all ingredients; mix well. Pour into prepared casserole dish.

3 Cover and bake 30 minutes. Uncover and bake 30 to 35 more minutes, or until set and top is golden. Spoon it up and enjoy!

Creamy Smashed Potatoes

Serves 6 to 8

4 pounds white potatoes, peeled and quartered

1/2 cup (1 stick) butter

1 cup sour cream

1/4 cup milk

1/2 teaspoon garlic powder

1-1/2 teaspoons salt

1 teaspoon black pepper

2 tablespoons fresh chives *or* scallions (green onions), sliced

1 Place potatoes in a soup pot and add enough water to cover them. Bring to a boil over high heat then reduce heat to medium and cook 15 to 20 minutes, or until fork-tender; drain and place in a large bowl.

2 Add remaining ingredients and whip potatoes with an electric beater until smooth.

3 Serve immediately, or place in a casserole dish and keep warm in a 250°F. oven for up to an hour before serving.

SERVING TIP: Want some extra crunch? Sprinkle on a can of French-fried onions right before serving.

Survival Meals

Cheeseburger Bake................................102

Italian Sandwich Bake..........................104

Ravioli Pesto Pie.................................105

Buffalo Chicken Pizza..........................106

Fancy Fast Chicken..............................108

Shortcut Beef Rollups..........................109

Garden Sloppy Joes.............................110

Fire Station Chili................................112

Cheeseburger Bake

Serves 4 to 6

*T*he kids will be home from school during the holidays, and with how much our budgets are being stretched now, we can make this dish that has everything they love about a cheeseburger — without the hefty tab of take-out.

1-1/2 pounds lean ground beef

1-1/2 teaspoons onion powder

1/2 teaspoon garlic powder

1/2 teaspoon black pepper

1/3 cup ketchup

1-1/2 cups (6 ounces) finely shredded sharp Cheddar cheese (see note)

1 (7.5-ounce) can refrigerated biscuits (10 biscuits)

1 Preheat oven to 450°F. Coat an 8-inch square baking dish with nonstick cooking spray.

2 In a large skillet, brown ground beef with onion powder, garlic powder, and pepper over high heat, stirring to break up beef. Drain off any fat then add ketchup and cheese; mix well then pour into baking dish.

3 Place biscuits over top and bake 8 to 10 minutes, or until biscuits are golden and baked through.

CHANGE IT UP: As always, any shredded cheese variety will do, so use your family's favorite.

Italian Sandwich Bake

Serves 4

*A*fter a hectic day at work or shopping, why not throw together this easy-as-can-be dinner-sized sandwich? While it's heating, you can probably wrap a few gifts or finish up those last-minute Christmas cards you've been meaning to get to.

4 ounces cream cheese, softened

2 tablespoons prepared pesto sauce

1 (16-ounce) ciabatta bread, cut in half horizontally (see note)

1/2 pound capicolla ham, thinly sliced

1/2 pound Genoa salami, thinly sliced

1/2 cup shredded mozzarella cheese

1 (12-ounce) jar roasted red peppers, drained, cut into 1/2" strips

1 teaspoon dried oregano

1 tablespoon grated Parmesan cheese

1 Preheat oven to 350°F.

2 In a medium bowl, combine cream cheese and pesto; mix well. Evenly spread pesto mixture on both sides of bread.

3 Evenly layer with capicolla then salami. Sprinkle with mozzarella then place red pepper strips over cheese. Sprinkle with oregano and Parmesan cheese then place top of bread back on sandwich and wrap sandwich in aluminum foil.

4 Bake 40 minutes, or until sandwich is heated through. Carefully unwrap sandwich then slice with a serrated knife and serve immediately.

CHANGE IT UP: If you'd rather, go ahead and use another type of crusty bakery bread and switch out the deli meats to your favorites.

Ravioli Pesto Pie

Serves 3 to 4

We may be in the holiday spirit these days but, with everybody running in so many directions, we could use something for dinner that boosts our overworked spirits. Keep these ingredients handy for an easy-as-pie meal that's like a combo of pizza and pasta.

1 (20-ounce) bag frozen cheese ravioli

1/2 cup (4 ounces) pesto sauce

1 (2-ounce) jar chopped pimientos

1/4 cup grated Parmesan cheese

1-1/2 ounces (about 25) pepperoni slices

1/2 cup (2 ounces) shredded mozzarella cheese

1 Preheat oven to 350°F. Boil ravioli according to package directions; drain.

2 In a large bowl, combine pesto, pimientos, Parmesan cheese, and pepperoni. Add ravioli and toss until evenly coated. Place in a 9-inch deep-dish pie plate and top with mozzarella cheese.

3 Cover loosely with aluminum foil and bake 20 to 25 minutes, or until cheese is melted and ravioli are heated through.

CHANGE IT UP: Go ahead and use different flavors of ravioli. It can be filled with meat, mushrooms, or even pesto.

NOTE: What's the best thing about survival dinners? They give us the gift of extra time to spend with the ones we love most!

Buffalo Chicken Pizza

Serves 4 to 6

*T*here are a load of reasons you'd want to make this, so, to start off, think "tree-trimming party." It delivers the taste of everybody's favorite chicken wings in the form of another party favorite: pizza! You can't go wrong — and everyone can easily help themselves.

1 (12-inch) prepared pizza crust (see Tips)

4 tablespoons (1/2 stick) butter, melted

1/4 cup hot cayenne pepper sauce (see Tips)

2 cups (1/2 pound) diced cooked chicken

1/2 cup chopped celery

1 cup (4 ounces) crumbled blue cheese

1/2 cup shredded mozzarella cheese

1 Preheat oven to 450°F. Coat a 12- to 14-inch pizza pan with nonstick cooking spray. Place pizza crust on pan.

2 In a medium bowl, combine butter and hot pepper sauce; mix well. Add chicken and celery; toss to coat well. Spread evenly over pizza crust then sprinkle with blue cheese and mozzarella cheese.

3 Bake 10 to 12 minutes, or until heated through and crust is crisp. Slice and serve.

TEST-KITCHEN TIPS: Use a shelf-stable pre-baked pizza crust and be sure to use hot *cayenne* pepper sauce, not hot pepper sauce. Yes, there is a difference and, boy, will your taste buds appreciate that you know the difference!

Fancy Fast Chicken

Serves 6

*T*his is one of my oldie-but-goodie recipes, and whether you've made it before or it's your first time, you'll agree it's a natural for busy nights. Who would guess something so "company fancy" could be this easy?

6 boneless, skinless chicken breast halves (1-1/2 to 2 pounds total)

6 (1-ounce) slices Swiss cheese

1 (10-3/4-ounce) can condensed cream of chicken soup

1/2 cup dry white wine

2 cups herb stuffing

2 tablespoons butter, melted

1 Preheat oven to 375°F. Coat a 9" x 13" baking dish with nonstick cooking spray.

2 Place chicken in prepared baking dish. Place a slice of cheese over each piece of chicken.

3 In a small bowl, combine soup and wine; mix well then pour over chicken. Sprinkle dry stuffing over chicken and drizzle with melted butter.

4 Bake 40 to 45 minutes, or until golden and no pink remains in chicken.

TEST-KITCHEN TIP: For added heartiness, top chicken with 1/4 pound sliced mushrooms (fresh, canned or jarred) before baking.

Shortcut Beef Rollups

Serves 4 to 6

*T*he supermarket deli counter truly is our best friend during these busy days leading up to Santa's visit. Keeping some versatile deli meat on hand means we can always come up with something good to eat, like these novel easy rollups.

3 cups warm prepared mashed potatoes (see Tip)

1 (16-ounce) package frozen mixed vegetables, thawed

12 thick slices deli roast beef (about 2 pounds)

1 (18-ounce) jar brown gravy

1 Preheat oven to 375°F.

2 In a large bowl, combine mashed potatoes and vegetables.

3 Place 1/3 cup potato mixture at smaller end of each roast beef slice and roll up crepe-style. Place beef rolls seam-side down in a large shallow roasting pan, making two rows of six.

4 Pour gravy over beef rolls then cover tightly with aluminum foil and bake 45 to 50 minutes, or until rolls are warmed through and gravy is bubbly.

TEST-KITCHEN TIP: This recipe's great for using leftover mashed potatoes (just warm them in the microwave first), but you can also use store-bought refrigerated mashed potatoes.

Garden Sloppy Joes

Serves 6

*T*his is the time of year we're always moaning about all the rich food we're about to indulge in at holiday gatherings. Here's a super weeknight meal that'll taste great and fill us up even though it's made with lighter ingredients so we can keep our waistlines from growing to Santa's size!

1-1/2 pounds ground turkey

1 large zucchini, chopped

1 medium-sized onion, chopped

1 large tomato, chopped

1 (26-ounce) jar spaghetti sauce

6 hamburger buns, split

1 In a large skillet, brown turkey, zucchini, and onion over medium-high heat for 10 to 12 minutes, or until no pink remains in turkey and zucchini is tender.

2 Reduce heat to medium-low and stir in tomato and spaghetti sauce. Cook 4 to 5 minutes, or until heated through. Spoon over buns and serve immediately.

CHANGE IT UP: Try serving these up on whole-grain buns. They add a nutty taste that makes your "Joes" really special.

Fire Station Chili

Serves 8 to 10

We've all heard that firefighters are known for their chili cookin', so I had to share one of their recipes. Don't be alarmed…it's not too hot, and it's a dinner that doesn't need much attention.

2 tablespoons vegetable oil

1 large onion, chopped

3 garlic cloves, minced

2 pounds ground beef

1 (28-ounce) can crushed tomatoes

1/3 cup chili powder

1 teaspoon salt

1 teaspoon ground cumin

1 teaspoon black pepper

2 (16-ounce) cans red kidney beans, drained

1 In a large pot, heat oil over medium-high heat and sauté onion and garlic for 5 minutes, or until tender.

2 Add ground beef and brown 8 to 10 minutes, or until no pink remains; drain off excess liquid.

3 Add remaining ingredients; mix well. Reduce heat to low, cover, and simmer for 30 minutes, stirring occasionally.

NOTE: If you want to give this a spicy kick, add 1 tablespoon hot pepper sauce along with the tomatoes.

SERVING TIP: It's fun to serve this in edible bread bowls. Just cut a small piece off the top of kaiser rolls, hollow them out, and divvy up the chili. Put out traditional chili toppers like shredded cheese, sour cream, chopped onions, and go to town!

Sweet Endings

Chocolate Mousse Cake......................114

Pumpkin Nut Torte...........................116

Pistachio Cake.................................117

Chocolate Snowballs.........................118

Chocolate Raspberry Cake..................119

Red Velvet Cake...............................120

No-Bake Eggnog Cheesecake..............122

Ricotta Cheesecake...........................123

Peppermint Swirl Cheesecake.............124

Jubilee Cherry Trifle.........................126

Holiday Panna Cotta.........................127

Snowman Cupcakes..........................128

Orange Bread Pudding......................130

Christmas Tree Brownie.....................131

Chocolate Pecan Pie.........................132

Italian Christmas Cream....................133

North Pole Cranberry Pie...................134

Minty Mousse.................................136

Chocolate Mousse Cake

Serves 12 to 16

*A*nyone who tastes this sinfully rich cake will be sure you hid a bakery box somewhere in your kitchen. When they realize you really made this heavenly chocolate dessert yourself, they'll be begging you for the recipe!

3 cups finely crushed chocolate graham crackers

1/2 cup (1 stick) butter, melted

2 eggs

4 egg yolks

3 cups semisweet chocolate chips

2 cups (1 pint) heavy cream

1/3 cup confectioners' sugar

1 In a medium bowl, combine crushed graham crackers and butter; mix well. Press into a 9-inch springform pan, covering bottom and sides to form a crust. Chill until ready to use.

2 In a small bowl, beat eggs and egg yolks; set aside. In a medium saucepan, melt chocolate chips over low heat, stirring constantly. Slowly add egg mixture, quickly whisking until well blended. Remove from heat; set aside to cool slightly.

3 Meanwhile, in a medium bowl, with an electric beater on medium speed, beat heavy cream until soft peaks form. Add confectioners' sugar and beat until stiff peaks form. Fold whipped cream into the slightly cooled chocolate mixture until well blended. Spoon into prepared crust; cover and chill at least 6 hours, or until firm.

SERVING TIP: Serve each slice with some fresh whipped cream and a chocolate-dipped strawberry. Wow!

Pumpkin Nut Torte

Serves 12 to 16

Move over, pumpkin pie, and say goodbye to run-of-the-mill desserts, 'cause this stacked creation is the perfect bring-along and a welcome change of pace on any holiday dessert buffet.

1 cup chopped walnuts

1 (18.25-ounce) package spice cake mix, batter prepared according to package directions

1 (16-ounce) can solid-pack pure pumpkin

3/4 cup confectioners' sugar

2 teaspoons ground cinnamon

1/2 teaspoon ground cloves

1/4 teaspoon ground nutmeg

1 (16-ounce) container frozen whipped topping, thawed

Whole walnuts for garnish (optional)

1 Stir chopped walnuts into prepared cake batter and bake according to package directions for two 9-inch round cake pans. Allow to cool completely on wire racks.

2 In a large bowl, combine pumpkin, confectioners' sugar, cinnamon, cloves, and nutmeg; mix well. Add whipped topping and mix well.

3 Using a sharp knife, carefully slice each cake layer in half horizontally, making a total of 4 cake layers. Place 1 cake layer cut-side down on a serving platter and top with one-fourth of the pumpkin mixture, spreading just to the edge. Repeat 3 more times with remaining cake layers and pumpkin mixture, ending with pumpkin mixture on top and leaving sides unfrosted.

4 Cover cake loosely and chill at least 3 hours before serving. Garnish top of cake with whole walnuts, if desired.

Pistachio Cake

Serves 12 to 16

*P*atty, my test-kitchen director, makes this cake as part of her family's Christmas tradition every year. Once she shared it with me, I knew I had to share it with you. *You can see how great the whole cake looks on the cover of the book!*

1 (18.25-ounce) package white cake mix

3 (4-serving) packages instant pistachio pudding and pie filling

1-1/2 cups milk, divided

1/2 cup vegetable oil

1/2 cup water

5 eggs

1 cup (1/2 pint) heavy cream

1/4 cup chopped pistachio nuts (optional)

1 Preheat oven to 350°F. Coat a Bundt pan with nonstick cooking spray then lightly flour.

2 In a large bowl, beat cake mix, 2 packages pudding mix, 1/2 cup milk, the oil, and water until smooth. Beat in eggs until well combined then pour into prepared Bundt pan.

3 Bake 55 to 60 minutes, or until a wooden toothpick inserted in center comes out clean. Cool 15 minutes then remove from pan and cool completely.

4 In a medium bowl, make frosting by beating heavy cream with the remaining 1 cup milk and package of pudding mix, until thickened; frost cake then garnish with chopped pistachio nuts, if desired.

Chocolate Snowballs

Makes 2 dozen

What's winter without snowballs...chocolate snowballs, that is? Go ahead and color some red, some green, some red and green, and maybe even leave some white.

1 (18.25-ounce) box chocolate cake mix, batter prepared according to package directions

4 cups sweetened flaked coconut

Red and green food color

1 (16-ounce) can white frosting

1 Preheat oven to 350°F. Spray 24 muffin cups with nonstick cooking spray and fill about 1/2 full with cake batter.

2 Bake 14 to 16 minutes, or until a wooden toothpick inserted in center comes out clean. Allow to cool 10 minutes then remove from muffin pans and place on cooling racks. Allow to cool completely then freeze cupcakes 2 hours, or until firm.

3 Meanwhile, to make colored coconut, add 2 to 3 drops food color to each 1 cup coconut in shallow bowls; mix well.

4 Frost top and sides of each cupcake with frosting. Sprinkle generously with colored coconut, patting gently to completely cover frosting. Serve immediately, or cover and let sit at room temperature until ready to serve.

Chocolate Raspberry Cake

Serves 12 to 15

Raspberries and chocolate...sounds like a combination you'd find at a fancy French restaurant, huh? But you can wow everybody at home with this scrumptious treat that's super-easy.

1 (12-ounce) container frozen whipped topping, thawed and divided

1/2 cup raspberry preserves

1 (9-ounce) package (about 40) chocolate wafer cookies

1/2 pint fresh raspberries

1 In a small bowl, combine half the whipped topping and the raspberry preserves; mix well. Spread 1 heaping teaspoon of the mixture on one side of each of 7 wafers, stacking the wafers on top of each other. Place a plain wafer on top.

2 Repeat, using remaining wafers and whipped topping mixture, making 5 stacks. Carefully turn each stack on its side and place them side by side on a platter. Frost with remaining whipped topping.

3 Freeze 3 to 4 hours, or overnight. If freezing overnight, make sure to cover well after whipped topping has set. When ready to serve, garnish with fresh raspberries, and slice.

HOW-TO: If you follow the step-by-step instructions and refer to these pictures, you'll be surprised just how easy this is.

Red Velvet Cake

Serves 12

*R*uby-colored red velvet cake, with its sinfully good cream cheese frosting, may have its roots in the south but it's sure to melt hearts from the North Pole to the South Pole with every velvety forkful.

1 (18.25-ounce) package butter flavored yellow cake mix

1/4 cup unsweetened cocoa

3/4 cup (1-1/2 sticks) butter, softened, divided

1 cup water

3 eggs

1 (1-ounce) bottle (2 tablespoons) red food color

1-1/2 cups confectioners' sugar

1 (8-ounce) package cream cheese, softened

1 tablespoon milk

1 Preheat oven to 350°F. Coat two 8-inch round cake pans with nonstick cooking spray.

2 In a large bowl, with an electric beater or medium speed, beat cake mix, cocoa, 1/2 cup butter, the water, and eggs until well combined. Add food color and beat until well combined. Pour batter into cake pans.

3 Bake 35 to 40 minutes, or until a wooden toothpick inserted in center comes out clean. Let cool 15 minutes then invert onto wire rack to cool completely. Using a sharp knife, carefully slice each cake in half horizontally, making a total of 4 cake layers.

4 In a medium bowl, with an electric beater or medium speed, beat confectioners' sugar, cream cheese, milk, and remaining 1/4 cup butter until well combined and smooth.

5 Place 1 cake layer cut-side down on a serving platter and top with one-fourth of the frosting, spreading just to the edge. Repeat 3 more times with remaining cake layers and frosting, ending with frosting on top and leaving sides unfrosted. Serve or cover loosely and chill until ready to serve.

GARNISHING TIP: Garnish top of cake with holiday sprinkles or decorating sugar to give it a festive look, if you'd like.

No-Bake Eggnog Cheesecake

Serves 9

*T*his recipe is perfect for the holidays, 'cause when your oven is stuffed with turkey, ham and all the trimmings, it's nice to know you have a cheesecake ready in the fridge that didn't need any baking!

3/4 cup graham cracker crumbs

1/2 cup sugar, divided

1/2 teaspoon ground nutmeg

1/4 cup (1/2 stick) butter, melted

1 (0.25-ounce) envelope unflavored gelatin

1/4 cup cold water

1 (8-ounce) package cream cheese, softened

1 cup eggnog

1 cup (1/2 pint) heavy cream

1 In a small bowl, combine graham cracker crumbs, 1/4 cup sugar, the nutmeg, and butter; mix well. Press into bottom of an 8-inch square baking dish; set aside.

2 In a small saucepan, combine gelatin and water; set aside 5 minutes to soften then stir over low heat 3 to 4 minutes, until gelatin is dissolved. Remove from heat and set aside.

3 In a large bowl, with an electric beater on medium speed, beat cream cheese and remaining 1/4 cup sugar until well blended. Stir in dissolved gelatin and eggnog, until well blended. Refrigerate 8 to 10 minutes, or until slightly thickened.

4 Whip the heavy cream then fold into gelatin mixture and pour over prepared crust; cover and chill 3 to 4 hours before serving.

Ricotta Cheesecake

Serves 8

What makes Italian-style cheesecake different from New York-style? The cheese! Instead of cream cheese, it uses ricotta cheese, which has a grainier texture and tangier flavor. It's a novel change of pace that your elves will surely welcome!

3/4 cup graham cracker crumbs

2 tablespoons butter, melted

1 (15-ounce) container part-skim ricotta cheese

1 cup plain low-fat yogurt

3/4 cup sugar

2 tablespoons all-purpose flour

2 tablespoons lemon juice

1 (8-ounce) package reduced-fat cream cheese, softened

2 eggs

2-1/2 teaspoons vanilla extract

1 Preheat oven to 350°F.

2 In a small bowl, combine graham cracker crumbs and melted butter; press into bottom and up sides of a 9-inch deep-dish pie plate. Bake 3 to 5 minutes, until lightly browned; let cool. (Leave the oven on.)

3 In a large bowl, with an electric beater on medium speed, combine ricotta cheese, yogurt, sugar, flour, and lemon juice until smooth; set aside.

4 In another large bowl, with beater on medium speed, beat cream cheese, eggs, and vanilla until thoroughly combined. Add ricotta mixture, beating on low speed until well combined; pour into pie crust.

5 Bake 60 to 65 minutes, or until center is nearly set. Cool 30 minutes then refrigerate overnight before serving.

GARNISHING TIP: Enjoy this plain or topped with fresh strawberry slices or whole blueberries or raspberries.

Peppermint Swirl Cheesecake

Serves 6 to 8

I used this recipe in one of my books about 10 years ago, and it was so popular that I had to include it in this collection because it's quick, easy, and rarely duplicated on holiday dessert tables.

2 (8-ounce) packages cream cheese, softened

1/2 cup sugar

2 eggs

3/4 cup sour cream

1 teaspoon vanilla extract

1 teaspoon peppermint extract

6 drops red food color

1 (9-inch) graham cracker pie crust

Whipped cream and miniature candy canes for garnish (optional)

1 Preheat oven to 350°F.

2 In a large bowl, beat cream cheese and sugar until light and fluffy. Add eggs and beat well. Add sour cream and vanilla; mix well.

3 Place 1/2 cup cream cheese mixture in a small bowl and stir in peppermint extract and red food color; mix well. Pour remaining cream cheese mixture into pie crust.

4 Drop peppermint cream cheese mixture by spoonfuls into cream cheese mixture and swirl with a knife to create a marbled effect.

5 Bake 30 to 35 minutes, or until the edges are firm (the center will be slightly loose).

6 Allow to cool 1 hour then cover and chill at least 6 hours before serving.

MAKE IT HOLIDAY-FESTIVE: Garnish each slice of cheesecake with a dollop of whipped cream or whipped topping and a miniature candy cane.

Jubilee Cherry Trifle

Serves 10 to 12

*T*rifles are some of the best desserts around at Christmas because they not only feed a bunch and everyone loves 'em, but they're the perfect centerpiece for any table.

1 (4-serving) package instant vanilla pudding and pie filling mix

2 cups milk

1 cup (1/2 pint) heavy cream

1 teaspoon vanilla extract

1/4 teaspoon ground ginger

2 (21-ounce) cans cherry pie filling

1 (16-ounce) pound cake, cut into 1-inch cubes

1 tablespoon chopped almonds

1 In a large bowl, whisk pudding mix and milk until thickened.

2 In another large bowl, combine heavy cream, vanilla, and ginger. Using an electric mixer, whip cream mixture until stiff peaks form. Gently fold whipped cream into pudding.

3 Spoon one-third of the cherry pie filling over the bottom of a trifle dish or large glass bowl. Layer with half the pound cake cubes then one-third of the cherry pie filling and half of the whipped cream mixture. Repeat layers once more, ending with a layer of whipped cream mixture.

4 Cover lightly and refrigerate at least 2 hours before serving. Garnish with chopped almonds.

Holiday Panna Cotta

Serves 6 to 8

*P*anna cotta is a chilled Italian-style dessert with a custard consistency. It may have a fancy name but this panna cotta recipe is easy as can be! It's ideal for individual desserts after a really big holiday meal.

1 (0.25-ounce) envelope unflavored gelatin

1/2 cup milk

2-1/2 cups heavy cream

1/2 cup sugar

2 teaspoons vanilla extract

1 In a small bowl, sprinkle gelatin over milk; let stand until gelatin is softened, about 5 minutes.

2 Meanwhile, in a large saucepan, combine heavy cream, sugar, and vanilla. Bring to a simmer over medium heat, stirring occasionally until sugar has dissolved. (Do not let it come to a boil.)

3 Remove mixture from heat, add softened gelatin mixture, and stir to completely dissolve the gelatin. Strain hot mixture into a large glass bowl then carefully pour or spoon mixture into custard cups.

4 Cover and refrigerate at least 6 hours, or overnight.

CHOCOLATE PISTACHIO PANNA COTTA: Make this decadent by topping with chopped pistachios and chocolate curls.

FRESH BERRY PANNA COTTA: For a fresh, light garnish, top with fresh berries (such as strawberries, raspberries or blueberries) just before serving.

Snowman Cupcakes

Serves 12 (Makes 2 adult and 3 kid snowmen)

*T*his adorable dessert is a fun recipe created and shared by my friends Alan Richardson and Karen Tack, authors of the hugely popular cookbooks "Hello, Cupcake!" and "What's New, Cupcake?" You can find more of their outrageous cupcake creations on MrFood.com and also on their site, hellocupcakebook.com.

1 cup sweetened flaked coconut, finely chopped

12 cupcakes, any flavor, unfrosted and baked in silver liners

1 (16-ounce) can vanilla frosting

4 orange slice candies

10 chocolate chips

1/4 cup mini chocolate chips

4 Famous chocolate wafers

13 thin pretzel sticks

6 spice drops

3 fruit slices

Fruit Stripe and Juicy Fruit gum

Additional candies: M&M's for buttons (regular and minis), candy sticks for canes, Sixlets (various sizes) and snow decors for snow

1 Place coconut in a shallow bowl. Frost top of each cupcake with a smooth mound of frosting then roll top of each in coconut to cover completely.

2 Arrange cupcakes on a serving platter or plates as shown. Make noses by cutting four 1" triangular pieces from each orange slice. Pinch one end of each to make them pointed. Add noses then press 2 chocolate chips, pointed ends in, above each nose to make eyes. Press mini chocolate chips, pointed ends in, below each nose to create smiles.

3 Add hats, bow ties, and earmuffs, plus additional candies for buttons, arms, canes, and snow.

FOR HATS: Using a serrated knife, cut a chocolate wafer into a 1-1/2" square. For brims: Cut 1/2" x 2" pieces from another wafer. Press a pretzel stick on an angle into top of each adult snowman's head to help support hat. Place square piece of wafer on top of pretzel support and into frosting at edge of cupcake to secure. Add brims to both hats.

FOR BOW TIES: Cut 1/2" from short end of gum. Pinch center of larger piece of gum together and wrap 1/2" trimmed piece around center. For scarf, trim gum into long narrow strips and shape by hand to create several wavy scarf pieces. Press pieces into cupcakes to secure.

FOR KIDS' EARMUFFS: Flatten 2 like-colored spice drops to 1-inch circles. Make 1/4" x 3" strips from outside edge of fruit slice by cutting a semi-circle from candy, leaving outer edge intact. Press strip into top edge of each kid snowman head to secure. Press a 2" pretzel piece into each flat side of spice drops and insert at end of fruit slice on either side of each cupcake.

Orange Bread Pudding

Serves 6 to 8

My test-kitchen team couldn't decide if this is a fruity side dish or a dessert. Well, I think this Dutch-inspired recipe teams well with poultry and ham, but I like it for dessert, too, so you decide how to serve it at your dinner.

13 slices white bread, cut into quarters

1-1/2 cups orange juice

1/4 cup (1/2 stick) butter

1 cup sugar

2 eggs

1/2 teaspoon grated lemon rind

1/4 teaspoon ground cinnamon

1 Preheat oven to 325°F. Coat a 1-1/2-quart baking dish with nonstick cooking spray.

2 In a large bowl, combine bread and orange juice, and beat with an electric mixer until smooth.

3 In a medium bowl, cream butter and sugar until light and fluffy; add remaining ingredients and mix until creamy. Add to bread mixture; mix well.

4 Pour into prepared baking dish and bake 1 hour, until center is set and puffy. Serve immediately.

TEST-KITCHEN TIP: This really is best when served right from the oven, drizzled with a bit of heavy cream.

Christmas Tree Brownie

Serves 10 to 12

While you're trimming the tree this year, why not dig into an edible brownie tree? After all, who doesn't like brownies?

1 (21.5-ounce) package brownie mix, batter prepared according to package directions

1 (16-ounce) can vanilla frosting

2 to 3 drops green food color

1/2 teaspoon mint extract

1 cup M&M's

1 junior-sized candy bar, unwrapped

MAKE IT HOLIDAY-FESTIVE: Line your serving platter with colored decorating sugar to make your cake sparkle.

1 Preheat oven to 350°F. Line a 9" x 13" baking pan with foil, extending foil over edges. Spray foil with nonstick cooking spray. Spread brownie batter evenly into pan and bake 25 to 30 minutes, or until a wooden toothpick inserted in center comes out clean. Cool brownies completely then freeze 30 minutes.

2 Using foil, lift brownies from pan and place on cutting board. To cut a tree shape from brownies, start at center of 1 short side, and make 2 diagonal cuts to corners of opposite short sides, forming a triangular piece in the center.

3 In a medium bowl, combine frosting, food color, and mint extract; mix well. Place 2 brownie side pieces together on a large serving tray to form a tree shape. Spread 1/3 cup frosting over top of tree shape. Stack with the whole tree shape, trimming if necessary to line up edges.

4 Frost sides and top of brownie tree with remaining frosting. Place M&M's decoratively over top of tree. Place candy bar at base of brownie tree to form a tree trunk.

Chocolate Pecan Pie

Serves 8

*P*ecan pie is so traditional that, at first, I was afraid to change it. I wasn't sure if I'd be able to improve upon something that's almost perfect. Boy, am I glad I tried, 'cause this chocolate version is sure to get plenty of "oohs" and "aahs"!

1 cup light corn syrup

1 cup packed light brown sugar

3 eggs

1 teaspoon vanilla extract

1-1/2 cups coarsely chopped pecans

3/4 cup (4-1/2 ounces) chocolate chips

1/4 cup (1/2 stick) butter, melted

1 (9-inch) frozen ready-to-bake pie shell, thawed

1 Preheat oven to 350°F.

2 In a large bowl, combine corn syrup, brown sugar, eggs, and vanilla; stir with a spoon until thoroughly mixed.

3 Add pecans, chocolate chips, and butter; mix well then pour into pie shell.

4 Bake 55 to 60 minutes, or until firm.

TEST-KITCHEN TIP: The filling in the center of the pie will settle a bit as it cools. Don't worry, it's supposed to!

Italian Christmas Cream

Serves 8 to 10

*T*his one's holiday-festive, smooth, and fresh-tasting. It's just what you need during the busy holiday season, 'cause it just takes mixing and freezing, but it tastes like a creamy, homemade Italian specialty. And, with all those colors, does it ever look great on your table!

2 medium-sized firm bananas,
   peeled and sliced

1 cup sliced seedless green grapes

2 cups (16 ounces) sour cream

1 cup coarsely chopped
   maraschino cherries

1 cup coarsely chopped walnuts

1/2 cup sugar

1-1/2 teaspoons grated fresh
   lemon peel

1 In a large bowl, combine all ingredients; mix well. Coat a 2-quart shallow casserole dish or mold with nonstick cooking spray. Pour mixture into prepared dish. Freeze overnight.

2 Before serving, let stand at room temperature for 15 to 20 minutes. (If using a mold, unmold onto a platter first.)

North Pole Cranberry Pie

Serves 8 to 10

Gotta make a fun pie this year for the company dessert party, or need something to bring to Grandma's to finish off your holiday dinner? This frozen pie will be very welcome...I promise!

1-1/2 cups graham cracker crumbs

3 tablespoons granulated sugar

1/2 cup (1 stick) butter, melted

1 (8-ounce) package cream cheese, softened

1 (16-ounce) can whole-berry cranberry sauce

1 (8-ounce) can crushed pineapple, drained and squeezed dry

1/2 cup chopped walnuts

1 cup sour cream

2 tablespoons light brown sugar

Fresh cranberries and mint sprigs (optional)

1 In a medium bowl, combine graham cracker crumbs, granulated sugar, and butter. Press into bottom and up sides of a 9-inch deep-dish pie plate, forming a crust.

2 In another medium bowl, with an electric mixer on low speed, beat cream cheese, cranberry sauce, pineapple, and walnuts until well combined. Spoon into pie crust.

3 In a small bowl, combine sour cream and brown sugar. Spoon over cranberry mixture, cover, and freeze at least 4 hours, or overnight.

4 Before slicing, let pie sit at room temperature for 20 to 30 minutes. Serve garnished with cranberries and fresh mint, if desired.

Minty Mousse

Serves 6 to 8

Make the end of a meal really stand out by serving homemade mousse. Its rich texture makes every spoonful scrumptious and luxurious.

1 (6-ounce) package white baking bars, broken up

2 cups (1 pint) heavy cream, divided

1-1/2 teaspoons mint extract

1/3 cup confectioners' sugar

8 drops green food color

1 In a medium saucepan, combine baking bars and 1/2 cup heavy cream over low heat, stirring constantly until bars are melted and mixture is smooth. Stir in mint extract then remove from heat and let cool completely.

2 In a medium bowl, with an electric beater on medium speed, beat sugar and remaining 1-1/2 cups cream until stiff peaks form. Add food color and continue beating until mixture is uniform in color.

3 Gently fold white chocolate mixture into whipped cream mixture until well blended. Spoon into serving dish, or individual serving glasses. Cover and chill at least 2 hours before serving.

GARNISHING TIP: Take this to the next level by topping with shaved white chocolate and fresh mint.

Cookies, Bars & More

Mistletoe Bars...138
Devilish Minty Cookies..............................140
Italian Christmas Cookies.........................141
Butter Cutout Cookies...............................142
Thumbprint Cookies...................................143
Apricot Macadamia Snowballs..............144
Ten-Minute Rum Balls...............................145
Linzer Tart Cookies....................................146
Almond-Kissed Cookies............................148
Church Windows..149
Pretzel Squares...150
Fruitcake Cookies.......................................151
Chocolate Snow Drops..............................152
Candy Cane Cookies..................................153
Pecan Tassies..154
Cheesecake Cookie Cups.........................156
Pecan Butter Balls......................................157
Oatmeal Raisin Bars..................................158
Snow-Topped Chocolate Bars..............159
Anise Biscotti...160
Gingerbread People...................................161
Peanut Butter Wrap-Arounds.................162

Mistletoe Bars

Makes 2 dozen

*M*eet your honey under the mistletoe...and be sure to have some of these in your hand for another sweet treat to share.

1 (18.25-ounce) package white cake mix

1/3 cup butter, melted

2 tablespoons water

2 eggs

1-1/2 cups dried cranberries

1 cup (6 ounces) white baking chips

1/2 cup cashews, coarsely chopped

1 Preheat oven to 350°F. Spray bottom only of a 9" x 13" baking dish with nonstick cooking spray, and lightly flour.

2 In a large bowl, using a spoon, combine cake mix, butter, water, and eggs until dough forms (some dry mix will remain). Stir in cranberries, baking chips, and cashews. Spread evenly in pan.

3 Bake 20 to 25 minutes, or until a wooden toothpick inserted in center comes out clean. Cool completely, about 1 hour, then cut into bars.

TEST-KITCHEN TIP: For an extra-special touch, melt 1/3 cup white baking chips with 1/2 teaspoon vegetable shortening over low heat, stirring frequently until melted and smooth. Place in a quart-sized plastic storage bag, snip a bit of one corner, and drizzle over each cooled bar. Let stand 30 minutes, or until set.

Devilish Minty Cookies

Makes 3 dozen

*A*dd some holiday cheer to your gatherings by baking a batch of these devilishly good chocolate cookies that'll wake up your taste buds with a burst of mint. *Turn back a page to see how great they look!*

1 (18.25-ounce) package devil's food cake mix

1/3 cup vegetable oil

2 eggs

3/4 cup coarsely chopped chocolate-covered thin mint candies

1 Preheat oven to 350°F. Coat baking sheets with nonstick cooking spray.

2 In a large bowl, combine cake mix, oil, and eggs; beat with an electric beater for 3 to 4 minutes, until well blended.

3 With a spoon, stir in chopped candies then drop by teaspoonfuls 2 inches apart onto prepared baking sheets.

4 Bake 9 to 11 minutes, or until cookies are firm. Remove cookies to a wire rack to cool completely.

CHANGE IT UP: Instead of mint candies, you can coarsely chop any of your favorite candy bars or nuts and mix them into the batter for even more variety.

Italian Christmas Cookies

Makes 4 dozen

W hat's a cookie platter or exchange without a few Italian-style Christmas cookies? Well, you'll be all set with these easy-to-make, fun-to-decorate, everybody-loves- 'em favorites. *See how festive these look in the photo on page 139.*

5 cups all-purpose flour

1 cup granulated sugar

5 teaspoons baking powder

1 cup vegetable oil

1 cup milk

Pinch of salt

2 teaspoons fresh lemon juice

2 eggs

Glaze:

3 cups sifted confectioners' sugar

4 tablespoons milk

Rainbow sprinkles and decorating
  sugar for topping (optional)

1 Preheat oven to 350°F. Coat baking sheets with nonstick cooking spray.

2 In a large bowl, combine flour, granulated sugar, baking powder, oil, milk, salt, lemon juice, and eggs. Roll dough into 1-inch balls and place on prepared baking sheets.

3 Bake 12 to 15 minutes, until cookies are set but not brown. Let sit 5 minutes then transfer to wire rack to cool completely.

4 In a medium bowl, combine glaze ingredients and stir until smooth.

5 Dip tops of cooled cookies in glaze and place on wire rack then immediately decorate as desired.

MAKE IT HOLIDAY-FESTIVE: If you want to decorate your cookies with multiple colors, separate glaze into smaller bowls and mix in food colors one drop at a time until reaching desired colors. If you want to add a flavor to your glaze, add a drop of your favorite extract.

Butter Cutout Cookies

Makes 4 to 6 dozen

Decisions, decisions. Which cookie cutter should you use first — the Christmas tree, the snowman or one of the others that you keep stashed deep down in your kitchen drawers? Make some of whatever ones you find!

1-1/2 cups (3 sticks) butter (see Tips)

1 cup sugar

1 egg

2 teaspoons vanilla extract

1/4 teaspoon salt

4-1/2 cups all-purpose flour

1 In a large bowl, beat butter, sugar, egg, vanilla, and salt with an electric mixer. Gradually add flour then beat until well combined. Refrigerate dough for 1 hour.

2 Preheat oven to 375°F.

3 Meanwhile, separate dough into 4 equal pieces then roll out each piece on a lightly floured surface to 1/4-inch thickness. Cut dough into desired shapes; place shapes on ungreased baking sheets.

4 Bake 8 to 10 minutes, or until light brown.

TEST-KITCHEN TIPS: It's best not to substitute margarine for butter in this recipe. Also, the size of the cookie cutters you use will determine the yield. (That's why we give such a wide range!) Have a ball decorating these with icing, sprinkles or whatever!

Thumbprint Cookies

Makes about 2 dozen

*T*alk about "hands on" baking! When they were little, my kids loved to press their little thumbs into these cookies. Yours will, too, so gather them together and create some tasty memories of your own by making these classic holiday cookies.

1 cup sugar

1/2 cup (1 stick) butter (see Tips)

1 egg

2 teaspoons vanilla extract

2 cups all-purpose flour

2 tablespoons milk

1/2 cup finely chopped walnuts

1/4 to 1/3 cup fruit preserves for filling (see Tips)

1 Preheat oven to 350°F. Coat baking sheets with nonstick cooking spray.

2 In a large bowl, using an electric beater, combine sugar, butter, egg, and vanilla. Add flour and milk; mix well.

3 Shape into balls then roll balls in chopped walnuts. Place on prepared baking sheets. Press thumb into center of each cookie ball to make an indentation then fill each "imprint" with your favorite preserves.

4 Bake 15 to 20 minutes, or until light golden.

TEST-KITCHEN TIPS: It's best not to substitute margarine for butter in this recipe. The amount of preserves you'll use will depend upon the size of your thumbprints! And be sure to use preserves, 'cause jams and jellies tend to liquefy while baking.

Apricot Macadamia Snowballs

Makes 2 dozen

What a fun way to decorate the table and serve a wintry treat at the same time! These no-bake goodies are sure to become an annual guest at your holiday get-togethers.

6 ounces dried apricots

1/4 cup apricot jam

1 tablespoon sugar

1 cup macadamia nuts

1/2 cup sweetened flaked coconut (see Tip)

1 In a food processor, blend apricots, jam, sugar, and nuts, pulsing until mixture forms a mass.

2 Form rounded teaspoonfuls of the mixture into 1-inch balls; roll each ball in coconut until well coated. Chill 1 hour before serving.

TEST-KITCHEN TIP: If you prefer a nuttier flavor, you can toast the coconut before using it. Just spread it out on a baking sheet and place the sheet in a 300°F. oven for a few minutes, until the coconut is light golden. Watch it carefully so it doesn't burn!

Ten-Minute Rum Balls

Makes about 4 dozen

Whatever's a Christmas celebration without rum balls? They're perfect served with a steamin' cup of coffee. Why, it's like your own version of cordials and coffee. Plus, they're extra-easy, 'cause you don't even have to bake 'em.

1 (11-ounce) package vanilla wafer cookies, finely crushed

1-1/2 cups finely chopped walnuts

1/2 cup light corn syrup

1/4 cup light *or* dark rum (see Tips)

1-1/2 cups confectioners' sugar, divided

1 In a large bowl, combine crushed cookies and walnuts; mix well. Stir in corn syrup and rum until thoroughly combined.

2 Place confectioners' sugar in a shallow dish. Roll cookie mixture into 1-1/2-inch balls. Roll in confectioners' sugar until completely coated (see Tips).

3 Serve, or store in an airtight container at room temperature until ready to serve.

TEST-KITCHEN TIPS: Out of rum? Add bourbon instead for a new twist on an old favorite. Also, these tend to absorb most of the confectioners' sugar after coating, so be sure to coat them very heavily; you might even want to roll them in additional sugar just before serving.

Linzer Tart Cookies

Makes 4 dozen

*T*hese bakery-worthy homemade layered butter cookies have a yummy jam filling that peeks through a cut-out center. They're pretty to look at, yummy to eat and perfect for cookie exchanges, not to mention bake sales and luncheons throughout the year.

1-1/2 cups (3 sticks) butter, softened

1 cup granulated sugar

1 egg

2 teaspoons vanilla extract

1/4 teaspoon salt

4-1/2 cups all-purpose flour

3/4 cup jam *or* preserves
   (see note)

1/4 cup confectioners' sugar

1 In a large bowl, with an electric beater on medium speed, beat butter, granulated sugar, egg, vanilla, and salt until creamy. Gradually add flour, beating until well mixed. Cover and chill 1 hour.

2 Preheat oven to 375°F.

3 Divide dough into 4 equal pieces. On a lightly floured surface, using a rolling pin, roll out each piece to 1/8-inch thickness. Using a 2-inch round cookie cutter, cut out circles and place 1 inch apart on ungreased cookie sheets. Using a canape cutter, a sharp knife, a 1-inch round cookie cutter, or a water bottle cap, cut out 1-inch circles or small shapes from the center of half of the cookies.

4 Bake cookies 10 to 12 minutes, or until light golden. Remove to wire racks to cool completely.

5 Spread jam evenly over the solid cookies. Sprinkle remaining cookies with confectioners' sugar. Place cookies with cutouts over jam-topped cookies. Serve, or store in an airtight container.

CHANGE IT UP: Any flavor jam can be used, but I like to use an assortment so there are different colors peeking through the holes in the cookie tops.

Almond-Kissed Cookies

Makes about 4 dozen

*A*lmond cookies are a popular light dessert for people of many cultures, so don't miss making them for your holiday cookie exchange and adding them to all your holiday cookie platters.

1 cup (2 sticks) butter, softened

1 cup sugar

1 egg

4 teaspoons almond extract (see Tip)

2-1/2 cups all-purpose flour

1-1/2 teaspoons baking soda

1/2 teaspoon salt

1/3 cup blanched almonds

1 Preheat oven to 350°F. Coat baking sheets with nonstick cooking spray.

2 In a medium bowl, with an electric beater on medium speed, cream butter and sugar. Add egg and almond extract; mix well. Add flour, baking soda, and salt; beat until well combined and dough is stiff.

3 Roll into 1-inch balls and place on baking sheets. Flatten slightly and push an almond lightly into the top of each cookie.

4 Bake 8 to 10 minutes, or until light golden. Remove to a wire rack to cool completely.

TEST-KITCHEN TIP: You can add a little more or less almond extract, depending on how "almondy" you want the cookies to be.

Church Windows

Makes about 2 dozen

*B*righten up holiday cookie trays with the colors of church windows! This is one of my all-time most-requested Christmas cookie recipes. These are really eye-catching, so consider this bonus recipe my holiday gift to you. Whether you've tried these before or not, they'll be at your fingertips right here!

1/2 cup (1 stick) butter, softened

1 (12-ounce) package (2 cups) semisweet chocolate chips

1 teaspoon vanilla extract

1 cup chopped walnuts

1 (10.5-ounce) bag multi-colored mini marshmallows

1 cup sweetened flaked coconut, divided

1 In a large saucepan, melt butter and chocolate chips over low heat until completely melted. Remove saucepan from heat and stir in vanilla and walnuts.

2 Cool mixture about 15 minutes, until cool but not to the point of hardening. Fold in marshmallows and stir until well coated.

3 Sprinkle 1/2 cup coconut over a 12-inch piece of wax paper. Spoon half the mixture lengthwise down the center of the wax paper. Shape into a 12" x 2" log and place at one edge of wax paper. Roll log over coconut, evenly coating outside of entire log. Wrap log firmly in wax paper, folding ends snugly.

4 Repeat with the other half of the marshmallow mixture and 1/2 cup coconut. Refrigerate until firm, at least 2 hours or overnight. Unwrap each log and cut into 1/4-inch slices.

Pretzel Squares

Makes about 4 dozen

*T*he contrast of sweet and salty tastes, and creamy and crunchy textures, make this easy dessert bar a crowd-pleaser! No matter how they like it, we've got them covered!

1 cup crushed pretzels

1/4 cup plus 1/3 cup butter, melted

1 (14-ounce) can sweetened condensed milk

1/4 cup sugar

1 cup (6 ounces) semisweet chocolate chips, melted (see Tip)

PREPARATION TIP: To melt chocolate chips, simply place in a small saucepan over medium-low heat and stir constantly just until melted and smooth.

1 Preheat oven to 400°F. Line a 7" x 11" baking pan with aluminum foil, letting ends extend beyond edges on two opposite sides. Coat foil with nonstick cooking spray.

2 In a small bowl, combine crushed pretzels and 1/4 cup melted butter; mix well then press into bottom of prepared pan. Bake 10 minutes; set aside.

3 In a small saucepan, combine sweetened condensed milk, sugar, and remaining 1/3 cup butter; bring to a boil over medium-high heat, stirring constantly. Reduce heat to medium-low and cook 10 minutes, or until golden, stirring constantly.

4 Pour sweetened condensed milk mixture over crust and chill 30 minutes, or until firm. Smooth chocolate over top and chill at least 2 hours, until firm.

5 Lift foil from pan then remove foil and place bars on a cutting board. Cut into small squares. Serve, or cover and keep chilled until ready to serve.

CHANGE IT UP: You can make these even more fun by pressing mini pretzels into the chocolate while still soft, so that each square has a pretzel on it.

Fruitcake Cookies

Makes about 4 dozen

*A*re you one of those people who turns up your nose at fruitcake? Trust me, this is no ordinary fruitcake. It's part cake, part cookie, and a whole lot of good taste. Unlike that fruitcake that gets passed around from house to house, these cookies are so yummy, they might not even make it out of your kitchen!

1 pound mixed candied fruit, diced (see Tip)

2 cups chopped pecans

2 cups all-purpose flour, divided

1/4 cup (1/2 stick) butter, softened

1 cup packed light brown sugar

2 eggs

1/4 cup milk

1 tablespoon baking powder

1/2 teaspoon ground cinnamon

1/2 teaspoon ground nutmeg

1 Preheat oven to 325°F. Coat baking sheets with nonstick cooking spray.

2 In a large bowl, combine candied fruit, nuts, and 1/2 cup flour. Toss until evenly coated; set aside.

3 In another large bowl, cream butter and brown sugar until fluffy. Beat in eggs and milk. Add remaining 1-1/2 cups flour, the baking powder, cinnamon, and nutmeg, and beat until well blended. Stir in fruit mixture; mix well and drop by rounded teaspoonfuls 1 inch apart onto prepared baking sheets.

4 Bake 15 to 18 minutes, or until golden. Remove to a wire rack to cool completely.

TEST-KITCHEN TIP: Mixed candied fruit can include a combination of pineapple, red and green cherries, and citron or, if you prefer, just use one of your favorites.

Chocolate Snow Drops

Makes about 5 dozen

*S*atisfy your sweet tooth with these heavenly cookies that are like a winter wonderland for your taste buds!

1 (1-pound 2-ounce) package cream-filled chocolate sandwich cookies

1 (8-ounce) package cream cheese, softened

1 (1-pound 8-ounce) package vanilla flavored almond bark (see Tips)

1 Coat a baking sheet with wax paper.

2 In a food processor, finely crush sandwich cookies. Add cream cheese and process until thoroughly mixed. Roll into 1/2-inch balls and place on a wax paper-lined baking sheet. Freeze 30 minutes.

3 Place almond bark in a large microwave-safe bowl and microwave 1 minute. Stir almond bark and continue to microwave at 15-second intervals until candy is melted and smooth. Do not overheat.

4 Using a toothpick to hold onto the chocolate balls, dip each ball into melted candy until evenly coated. Shake off excess coating and place on prepared baking sheet. Keep refrigerated.

TEST-KITCHEN TIPS: You may substitute almond bark with 4 (6-ounce) packages of white baking bars. Also, if you want to decorate these with sprinkles or colored sugar, be sure to do so before the candy coating hardens, or the decorations won't stick.

Candy Cane Cookies

Makes about 4 dozen

We've got the perfect use for all those broken candy canes, and we're betting that Santa would agree that these jolly cookies are a huge hit! Delivering lots of smiles and tons of holiday cheer, they're a must-have this season!

1 cup (2 sticks) butter, softened

1 cup confectioners' sugar

1 egg

1/2 teaspoon peppermint extract

1/2 teaspoon vanilla extract

2-1/2 cups all-purpose flour

1/4 teaspoon salt

1 cup crushed candy canes

3 tablespoons granulated sugar

1 Preheat oven to 375°F.

2 In a large bowl, cream butter and confectioners' sugar until light and fluffy. Add egg and the peppermint and vanilla extracts, and beat until well blended. Gradually add flour and salt; mix well. Cover bowl tightly with plastic wrap and chill 1 hour.

3 Coat two baking sheets with nonstick cooking spray. In a shallow bowl, combine crushed candy canes and the granulated sugar; mix well.

4 Shape chilled dough into 1-inch balls then roll each ball in candy cane mixture; place on prepared baking sheets.

5 Bake 10 to 12 minutes, or until browned. Immediately remove from baking sheets and place on wire racks to cool.

PREPARATION TIP: Don't have any candy canes? No problem! You can use 1 cup crushed peppermint hard candies.

Pecan Tassies

Makes 2 dozen

My wife made these treats all the time when our family was young. A favorite in our Upstate New York home, these little mini tarts with a cream cheese crust are a regular treat in the deep south. They'll surely please your gang, no matter what part of the country you live in!

1/2 cup (1 stick) plus 1 tablespoon butter, softened, divided

1 (3-ounce) package cream cheese, softened

1 cup all-purpose flour

1/2 cup packed light brown sugar

1 egg

1 teaspoon vanilla extract

1/8 teaspoon salt

1/2 cup coarsely chopped pecans

1 In a large bowl, with an electric beater on medium speed, beat 1/2 cup butter and the cream cheese until creamy. Add flour, beating until mixture is well combined. Cover and chill dough 30 minutes.

2 Preheat oven to 325°F.

3 In another large bowl, combine remaining ingredients, including the remaining 1 tablespoon butter; stir until well combined.

4 Shape chilled dough into 24 one-inch balls. Place each dough ball into an ungreased mini muffin cup. Using your thumb, press the dough to form a crust. Spoon pecan mixture into each indentation in dough, filling them three-fourths full.

5 Bake 35 to 40 minutes, or until filling is firm and crust is golden. Cool slightly then remove to a wire rack to cool completely.

6 Serve warm, or cover and chill until ready to serve.

Cheesecake Cookie Cups

Makes 2 dozen

"*A*wesome!" "The best!" These are just a few of the rave reviews these got from my grandchildren. They just loved getting their very own cheesecakes! *You won't be able to resist these either when you turn back a page to check them out.*

1 (18-ounce) package refrigerated chocolate chip cookie dough

1 (8-ounce) package cream cheese, softened

1/3 cup sugar

1/2 teaspoon vanilla extract

1/2 teaspoon unsweetened cocoa

1 Preheat oven to 375°F. Coat mini muffin cups with nonstick baking spray.

2 Slice cookie dough into 24 slices. Roll each slice into a ball and place in prepared muffin cups. Press down in center to make a deep well.

3 Bake 10 to 12 minutes, or until edges are set and "crusts" are golden. Remove from oven and press down in center with a spoon to make an indentation. Let stand 5 minutes then remove to wire racks to cool completely.

4 In a small bowl, with an electric beater on medium speed, beat cream cheese, sugar, and vanilla until smooth. Spoon 1 teaspoon cream cheese mixture into each cup. Dust tops with cocoa (see note) and serve.

CHANGE IT UP: Instead of dusting these with cocoa, you might want to top them with some cherry pie filling for a mini cherry cheesecake treat that kids of any age will love!

156

Pecan Butter Balls

Makes about 2 dozen

Mmm, these have a rich, buttery taste, and they're studded with chopped pecans. What could be better than this melt-in-your-mouth cookie?

1/4 cup plus 2 tablespoons sugar, divided

1 cup finely chopped pecans

1 teaspoon vanilla extract

3/4 cup (1-1/2 sticks) butter, softened

1/8 teaspoon salt

1 cup all-purpose flour

1 Place 1/4 cup sugar in a shallow pan and set aside.

2 In a large bowl, combine 2 tablespoons sugar and remaining ingredients. With your hands, mix until thoroughly blended; cover and refrigerate dough 30 minutes.

3 Preheat oven to 375°F.

4 Meanwhile, form dough into 1-1/4-inch balls then roll in reserved sugar, covering completely. Place 1 inch apart on an ungreased baking sheet.

5 Bake 15 to 20 minutes, or until set but not brown. Let stand 1 minute. Remove to a wire rack to cool.

Oatmeal Raisin Bars

Makes 21

*T*he wholesome goodness of oatmeal turns these snack bars into a healthy option! Bake up a batch and feel good about serving these mouthwatering treats to your family and friends.

3/4 cup (1-1/2 sticks) butter

1 tablespoon maple *or* maple flavored syrup

1 teaspoon baking soda

1/2 teaspoon ground allspice

2 cups quick-cooking *or* old-fashioned rolled oats

1 cup all-purpose flour

1 cup sugar

1/4 cup raisins

1 Preheat oven to 350°F. Coat a 9" x 13" baking dish with nonstick cooking spray.

2 Melt butter and syrup over low heat on stovetop or in microwave. Transfer mixture to a large bowl and add baking soda and allspice; mix well and let cool.

3 Add rolled oats, flour, sugar, and raisins; mix well. Press dough into prepared baking dish.

4 Bake 15 minutes. Immediately cut into bars while still warm but do not remove from dish; let cool completely then cut again along same lines before removing.

Snow-Topped Chocolate Bars

Makes about 3 dozen

Whether it's a white Christmas or not, these "snow-topped" goodies will bring a ray of sunshine to everyone's faces.

1 (12-ounce) package (2 cups) semisweet chocolate chips

1 (8-ounce) package cream cheese, softened

1 (5-ounce) can evaporated milk

1/2 cup chopped walnuts

1 teaspoon almond extract, divided

3 cups all-purpose flour

1-1/2 cups granulated sugar

1 teaspoon baking powder

1/2 teaspoon salt

1 cup (2 sticks) butter, softened

2 eggs

1/2 teaspoon vanilla extract

1 tablespoon confectioners' sugar

1 Preheat oven to 350°F.

2 In a medium saucepan, combine chocolate chips, cream cheese, and evaporated milk. Heat over low heat, stirring constantly, until chips are melted and mixture is smooth. Remove from heat. Add nuts and 1/2 teaspoon almond extract; blend well and set aside.

3 In a large bowl, combine flour, granulated sugar, baking powder, salt, butter, eggs, vanilla, and the remaining almond extract. Beat with an electric mixer on low speed until mixture resembles coarse crumbs.

4 Press half of the crumb mixture into an ungreased 9" x 13" baking dish. Spread chocolate mixture over crumb mixture. Sprinkle with remaining crumb mixture (see Tip).

5 Bake 35 to 40 minutes, or until golden. Cool, sprinkle with confectioners' sugar then cut into bars.

TEST-KITCHEN TIP: The top layer should be a crumby texture. If the dough for the top layer gets soft, pinch off small pieces and place them on top of the chocolate that way.

Anise Biscotti

Makes about 3-1/2 dozen

*B*iscotti has to be one of the trendiest cookies around. From what we can tell, it's the crunch that really attracts everyone to biscotti, so make sure you follow the instructions to get the perfect crunch every time. By the way, including anise in here gives these their authentic Italian flavor.

3 cups all-purpose flour

2 cups sugar

1/2 teaspoon salt

1 teaspoon baking powder

4 eggs

1 teaspoon anise extract

1 Preheat oven to 350°F. Coat two large baking sheets with nonstick cooking spray.

2 In a large bowl, combine all ingredients; mix well and, using your hands, work dough until it forms a ball. Place half the dough on one baking sheet and form into a 3" x 12" loaf about 1 inch high. Repeat with remaining dough on second baking sheet.

3 Bake 25 to 30 minutes, or until firm and light golden. Remove from oven and reduce heat to 325°F.

4 Allow loaves to cool 5 minutes. Cut into 1/2-inch slices and place cut-side down on baking sheets.

5 Bake cookies 15 minutes then turn them over and bake 15 more minutes, or until very crisp. Allow to cool, then serve, or store in an airtight container.

Gingerbread People

Makes 2 dozen 7-inch cookies

*T*he holidays aren't official unless somebody makes gingerbread cookies. These are a seasonal treat every little elf looks forward to.

1-1/2 cups molasses

1 cup packed brown sugar

2/3 cup cold water

1/3 cup butter, softened

6 cups all-purpose flour

2 teaspoons baking soda

1 teaspoon salt

1 teaspoon ground allspice

2 teaspoons ground ginger

1 teaspoon ground cloves

1 teaspoon ground cinnamon

1 In a large bowl, combine molasses, brown sugar, water, and butter. Add remaining ingredients and blend well. Cover and refrigerate 2 hours.

2 Preheat oven to 350°F. Coat baking sheets with nonstick cooking spray. Divide dough in half. On a lightly floured surface, roll dough to 1/2-inch thickness. Cut with gingerbread people cookie cutters and place on prepared baking sheets (see Tips).

3 Bake 10 to 12 minutes. Remove to wire racks and cool then decorate as desired (see Tips).

TEST-KITCHEN TIPS: If you'd like to use raisins for eyes and red cinnamon candies for buttons, press them lightly into dough before baking. This dough will hold well in the refrigerator for a few days, so you can make it in advance, at your convenience, then bake up the fresh cookies when you want 'em.

Peanut Butter Wrap-Arounds

Makes about 2 dozen

*F*or a tasty marriage made in heaven, deck out your holiday cookie tray with chocolate kisses wrapped in peanut butter. It's a pairing that'll have everyone going "nuts." (You'd better make a double batch!)

1 cup sugar

1 cup creamy peanut butter

1 egg

1 teaspoon vanilla extract

24 to 30 chocolate candy kisses, unwrapped

1 Preheat oven to 325°F.

2 In a medium bowl, combine sugar, peanut butter, egg, and vanilla; mix well. Wrap a heaping teaspoon of dough completely around each piece of chocolate.

3 Bake on ungreased baking sheets for 13 to 15 minutes, or until light golden. Let cool before removing from baking sheets.

CHANGE IT UP: For a tasty change of pace, make a festive variety of batches using almond and white chocolate candy kisses, too!

Santa's Sippers

Caramel Latte.....................................164

Whipped Cream Dollops.......................164

Hot Spiced Cider...................................166

Pineapple Wassail.................................166

S'mores Hot Cocoa...............................167

White Christmas Eggnog.......................167

Pomegranate Sangria............................168

Cocoa Peppermint Frosty.....................170

Caramel Latte

Serves 1 (makes 1-3/4 cups)

When my wife Ethel comes home after hours of holiday shopping, she drops her packages and sits for a few minutes with a cup of this Caramel Latte. It's her reward for standing in those endless lines at the mall. She sure loves it, and so will you!

1-1/2 cups hot brewed coffee

3 teaspoons sugar

1/2 teaspoon vanilla extract

1/4 cup warm milk

1/4 cup caramel sauce, divided

Whipped cream or Whipped Cream Dollops (see recipe below)

1 Fill a mug with the coffee; stir in sugar, vanilla, and warm milk.

2 Stir in 3 tablespoons caramel sauce; mix well. Top with prepared whipped cream or whipped topping, or a whipped cream dollop (see below) and drizzle with remaining caramel sauce.

Whipped Cream Dollops

Makes 2 dozen

1/2 pint (8 ounces) heavy cream

2 teaspoons confectioners' sugar

1 In a medium bowl, whip cream and sugar with an electric beater on high speed for 3 to 5 minutes, or until soft peaks form (and hold together like real whipped cream is supposed to).

2 Spoon heaping teaspoon-sized dollops of whipped cream onto a wax paper-lined baking sheet. Freeze 1-1/2 hours, or until solid. Transfer dollops to a plastic bag, close tightly, and store in freezer until ready to use. Just before serving, remove one dollop per latte or other dessert and allow to thaw before using. (These thaw in minutes and will last in the freezer for up to 1 month.)

Hot Spiced Cider

Serves 6 to 8 (makes about 1/2 gallon)

*I*t just wouldn't be Christmas without a mug of hot cider on a frosty winter night! This is the perfect "sit by the fire" sipper that should be part of the magical memories of the holiday season.

1/2 gallon apple cider

1 orange, sliced

1/4 cup packed light brown sugar

2 cinnamon sticks

2 teaspoons whole cloves

1 In a large pot, bring all ingredients to a boil over medium-high heat. Reduce heat to low and simmer 10 minutes. Serve hot. Chill any leftovers and microwave to heat as needed.

Pineapple Wassail

Serves 8 to 10 (makes about 2-1/2 quarts)

*W*assail! Every year you hear carolers sing about it, but what *is* wassail? It's a steaming hot fruit punch that's a centuries-old holiday tradition. Imagine enjoying it after a night of caroling yourself.

1 (46-ounce) can pineapple juice

2 (12-ounce) cans frozen orange juice concentrate, thawed

2 cups water

3/4 cup corn syrup

2 teaspoons fresh lemon juice

4 cinnamon sticks

4 whole cloves

1 In a soup pot, bring all ingredients to a boil over high heat. Reduce heat to low, cover loosely, and simmer 30 minutes, stirring occasionally.

2 Remove cinnamon sticks and cloves then pour into mugs and serve hot.

TEST-KITCHEN TIP: These are great made in and served from a slow-cooker. Not only do they stay hot and ready to serve, but they fill the house with comforting aromas.

166

S'mores Hot Cocoa

Serves 4

*H*ot cocoa brings out the kid in all of us, especially this one that has all the tastes of our summertime campfire favorite...s'mores! Imagine the look on the faces of your kids and all the kids-at-heart in your house when they get a sip of this!

4 cups hot cocoa (see Tip)

1/2 cup marshmallow crème

1/4 cup coarsely crushed
   graham crackers

1 Pour hot cocoa into 4 mugs.

2 Evenly top each mug of cocoa with marshmallow crème and graham cracker crumbs. Serve immediately.

TEST-KITCHEN TIP: Use your favorite mix to make the hot cocoa or, for every mug of S'mores Hot Cocoa, heat 8 ounces milk with 2 tablespoons chocolate flavor syrup.

White Christmas Eggnog

Serves 4 to 6

*W*e all have holiday memories that center around traditional foods and drinks. I bet rich 'n' creamy eggnog is near the top of your list — it's on mine. And with this version, kissed with chocolate liqueur, whatever the weather, it's going to be a white Christmas at your house!

2 cups prepared (canned or
   refrigerated) eggnog, chilled

3/4 cup white chocolate liqueur

1/4 cup rum or whisky

Nutmeg for sprinkling

1 In a pitcher, combine eggnog, liqueur, and rum; stir until thoroughly combined.

2 Pour into cocktail glasses and garnish with nutmeg. Serve immediately.

Pomegranate Sangria

Serves 8 to 10

While the kids are outside building a snowman, we grown-ups can have our own good time with this trendy version of classic fruity sangria. The pomegranate juice not only adds a refreshing twist but it's also good for us, so why not indulge and enjoy...responsibly, of course.

1 (6-ounce) container frozen limeade concentrate, thawed

1 (6-ounce) container frozen lemonade concentrate, thawed

3 cups pomegranate juice

3 cups Burgundy *or* other dry red wine

1 cup cold water

1 lime, washed and thinly sliced

1 orange, washed and thinly sliced

Ice cubes

Pomegranate seeds for garnish (optional)

1 In a large pitcher or punch bowl, combine limeade and lemonade concentrates, pomegranate juice, wine, and water; stir until well combined.

2 Stir in lime and orange slices, and serve in ice-filled tall glasses or wine glasses. Garnish with pomegranate seeds, if you'd like.

TEST-KITCHEN TIP: Make an ice mold to float in your punch bowl of sangria. That'll keep it chilled just right all night long.

Cocoa Peppermint Frosty

Serves 4

I know you're probably thinking that a frosty milkshake is a surprising suggestion for wintertime. Well, whether you're a year-round ice cream eater, or if you live in a warm climate and crave the tastes of the holiday season, this one's a sensational sipper you won't want to miss.

6 red-and-white peppermint hard candies, unwrapped

2 tablespoons sugar

2 tablespoons unsweetened cocoa

2 cups milk, divided (see note)

1 large scoop vanilla ice cream (see note)

1 Place candies in a blender, cover, and blend until finely crushed. Be sure all candy is finely crushed.

2 Add sugar, cocoa, and 1 cup milk; blend well. Add remaining milk and the ice cream. Blend until smooth and creamy. Serve immediately.

CHANGE IT UP: If you want to enjoy a lower-fat version, use skim milk and low-fat frozen yogurt or ice cream, and it will still be a smooth and creamy treat. And if you want, you can switch the vanilla ice cream for peppermint ice cream for an even more intense minty taste!

Gifts from the Kitchen

Sugar 'n' Spice Nuts.............................172

Cranberry Clusters.............................172

Chocolate Almond Bonbons.................174

Red Cinnamon Popcorn.......................175

Gingerbread Play Dough.....................175

Brickle Crunch....................................176

Macadamia Turtles.............................177

Chocolate Chip Cranberry Bread........178

Munch and Crunch.............................180

Chocolate Walnut Fudge.....................181

Butter Pecan Fudge............................182

Reindeer Fudge..................................184

Sugar 'n' Spice Nuts

Makes about 3 cups

*I*f you're looking for an edible gift that ships well, we've got two of 'em right here! Make one or both to send off to loved ones far away, and they'll taste the love you're sending at the holidays.

1 cup cashews

1 cup pecan halves

1 cup dry roasted peanuts

1 egg white, beaten slightly

1/4 cup packed light brown sugar

1/2 teaspoon ground cinnamon

1/4 teaspoon ground red pepper

1/2 cup dried cranberries

1 Preheat oven to 325°F. Coat a rimmed baking sheet with nonstick cooking spray.

2 In a large bowl, combine cashews, pecans, and peanuts. Add egg white and toss to coat nuts evenly.

3 In a small bowl, combine brown sugar, cinnamon, and ground red pepper; mix well then add to nut mixture. Stir until nuts are well coated then spread nuts onto baking sheet in a single layer.

4 Bake 18 to 20 minutes, or until lightly toasted, stirring halfway through cooking time. Let cool.

5 Mix dried cranberries into nuts; serve immediately, or store in an airtight container until ready to serve.

Cranberry Clusters

Makes about 2 dozen

2 tablespoons vegetable shortening

2 (6-ounce) packages white baking bars, cut into chunks (see note)

1 (12-ounce) package fresh cranberries, rinsed and dried

1 In a medium saucepan, melt shortening over low heat. Add baking bars and stir continuously until melted. Stir in cranberries then remove from heat.

2 Drop by heaping teaspoonfuls onto a wax paper-lined cookie sheet. Chill 2 hours, or until hardened.

3 Place in an airtight storage container and keep refrigerated until ready to serve.

CHANGE IT UP: Two cups of chocolate chips can be used instead of white baking bars.

172

Chocolate Almond Bonbons

Makes about 1 dozen

Share your passion for holiday candy by making a double batch of these yummy bonbons. Keep some on hand for your get-togethers then tuck the rest in decorative gift tins for spreading homemade Christmas cheer.

1-1/2 teaspoons instant coffee granules

1 tablespoon hot water

1-1/2 cups confectioners' sugar

4 (1-ounce) squares unsweetened chocolate, melted

1 (3-ounce) package cream cheese, softened

1/2 cup sliced almonds, finely chopped

1 In a medium bowl, dissolve coffee granules in water. Add remaining ingredients except almonds.

2 With an electric beater on medium speed, beat until smooth; cover and chill 30 minutes.

3 Roll into 1-inch balls then roll in chopped almonds, coating completely. Serve, or cover and chill until ready to serve.

CHANGE IT UP: These candies can also be coated in chocolate or colored sprinkles, confectioners' sugar, cocoa powder, or even other types of chopped nuts. What a pretty dessert platter you can make with some of each!

Red Cinnamon Popcorn

Makes 16 cups

*T*he kids are around the house more at holiday time, so mix up some fun with this colorful popcorn treat and homemade Gingerbread Play Dough. It'll be the start of magical holiday memories!

16 cups popped popcorn

1/2 cup butter

1/2 cup light brown sugar

1/4 cup light corn syrup

1/2 teaspoon vanilla extract

3/4 cup red cinnamon candies

1/4 teaspoon baking soda

2 tablespoons green candy sprinkles

1 Place popped popcorn in a large bowl and set aside.

2 In a medium saucepan, melt butter over medium heat then stir in brown sugar, corn syrup, vanilla, and cinnamon candies. Bring to a boil and continue boiling until candy is dissolved, stirring constantly. Continue boiling for 3 more minutes then remove from heat and stir in baking soda.

3 Pour over popcorn, mixing until evenly coated. Spread onto 2 foil-lined baking sheets and sprinkle immediately with green sprinkles; let cool.

4 Break apart and store in airtight containers or cellophane gift bags.

Gingerbread Play Dough

Makes 1-1/4 cups

1 cup all-purpose flour

1/2 cup salt

2 teaspoons cream of tartar

1 teaspoon ground cinnamon

1 teaspoon ground ginger

1 cup water

1 teaspoon vegetable oil

1 In a medium saucepan, combine all ingredients and cook over medium heat, stirring frequently.

2 When mixture begins to pull away from sides of pan, remove from heat and knead until smooth. Let cool. The kids can play with this and even taste it! It'll keep for a few weeks if stored in an airtight container.

Brickle Crunch

Makes 2 to 3 dozen pieces

*O*pposites attract, and the proof is in this salty-sweet, crunchy yet melt-in-your mouth brickle that is the perfect holiday gift for that certain hard-to-shop-for someone!

35 saltine crackers (about 1 sleeve from a 16-ounce box)

1 cup (2 sticks) butter

1 cup sugar

1 cup (6 ounces) semisweet chocolate chips

1 cup peanut butter chips

1 Preheat oven to 400°F. Line a 10" x 15" baking sheet with aluminum foil. Lay out crackers side by side on baking sheet.

2 In a medium saucepan, melt butter then add sugar and boil for 2 to 3 minutes, stirring frequently, until sugar is completely dissolved. Immediately pour mixture over crackers and bake 7 minutes.

3 Remove pan from oven and immediately sprinkle chocolate and peanut butter chips over crackers, spreading evenly as they melt (see Tip).

4 Let cool slightly. Refrigerate at least 30 minutes then break into pieces. Serve immediately, or refrigerate until ready to serve.

GARNISHING TIP: This is great topped with chopped nuts or flaked coconut; just sprinkle either on top immediately after spreading the chocolate and peanut butter chips.

Macadamia Turtles

Makes 2 dozen

In Hawaii, "Merry Christmas" is "Mele Kalikimaka." When you offer your guests this ooey-gooey, crunchy taste of tropical paradise on a chilly winter day, don't be surprised if they're inspired to say hello with the traditional Hawaiian holiday greeting!

3/4 to 1 pound macadamia nuts

1 (14-ounce) package caramels, unwrapped

3 tablespoons heavy cream

1 (12-ounce) package (2 cups) milk chocolate chips

1 tablespoon vegetable shortening

1 Cover 2 baking sheets with wax paper and coat with nonstick cooking spray. Arrange macadamia nuts into 24 groups on cookie sheets.

2 In a small saucepan, melt caramels with cream over low heat for 5 to 7 minutes, or until smooth, stirring constantly. Immediately spoon caramel mixture over each nut group while still hot; reheat caramel if it gets too thick.

3 In another small saucepan, melt chocolate chips with shortening over low heat for 5 to 7 minutes, or until smooth, stirring constantly. Drizzle chocolate over caramel-covered nuts (see Tip, page 138) and let stand until firm.

CHANGE IT UP: These will work with any type of nuts, so substitute your favorite and enjoy the contrasts of chewy and crunchy!

Chocolate Chip Cranberry Bread

Makes 2 loaves

*L*ooking for that "little something" to give your kids' teachers, your neighbors and your hair stylist? This one fits the bill, plus it tastes like a million bucks without breaking the bank.

2-1/2 cups all-purpose flour

1-1/2 cups sugar

1 tablespoon baking powder

1/2 cup vegetable shortening

3 eggs

1 cup cranberry juice cocktail

1/4 cup chocolate-flavored syrup

1 cup dried cranberries

1/2 cup (3 ounces) semisweet
   chocolate chips

1/2 cup chopped walnuts

1 Preheat oven to 350°F. Coat two 4" x 8" loaf pans with nonstick cooking spray.

2 In a large bowl, combine flour, sugar, and baking powder. With an electric beater, beat in shortening until well combined. Beat in eggs, cranberry juice, and chocolate syrup until thoroughly combined. Fold in cranberries, chocolate chips, and walnuts. Pour batter into prepared pans.

3 Bake 50 to 55 minutes, or until a wooden toothpick inserted in center comes out clean.

4 Cool 5 minutes before removing from pan then cool completely on a wire rack. Slice and serve as is or topped with butter.

CHANGE IT UP: Wanna bake these in mini loaf pans? Go ahead. Just reduce the cooking time accordingly, based on your pan size. For gift-giving, wrap a whole loaf or mini loaves in cellophane and tie with ribbon.

Munch and Crunch

Makes 16 cups

*H*ere's the plan: Make a batch of this then go to your local dollar store and pick up a bunch of holiday tins or mugs. Fill 'em up, wrap 'em up, and you'll be ready with a bunch of yummy gifts!

3 cups oven-toasted corn cereal

3 cups oven-toasted rice cereal

3 cups toasted oat cereal

1 (8-ounce) can salted peanuts

2 cups raisins

4 cups mini twist pretzels

1 (14-ounce) package red and green M&M's

1-1/2 pounds almond bark *or* white chocolate disks

1 In a large bowl, combine all ingredients except almond bark; mix well and set aside.

2 In a microwave-safe large bowl, melt almond bark for 1 minute; stir and continue heating for 15-second intervals until all bark is melted and smooth, stirring at each interval. DO NOT OVERHEAT. Pour over cereal mixture, stirring until evenly coated.

3 Spread mixture on 3 wax paper-lined baking sheets. Let cool then break into smaller pieces and store in airtight container.

MAKE-AHEAD TIP: Get a head start on your holidays by making batches of this in advance and storing them in airtight containers until ready to share and enjoy.

Chocolate Walnut Fudge

Makes about 3 dozen pieces

'*T*is the season to say "thank you" to your kids' teachers. Go old school by gifting them with a batch of old-fashioned homemade fudge. Betcha this treat will send your kids straight to the head of the class!

2 (14-ounce) cans sweetened condensed milk

1 (12-ounce) package semisweet chocolate chips

1 (12-ounce) package milk chocolate chips

1 cup chopped walnuts

1 In a medium saucepan, bring sweetened condensed milk to a rolling boil over medium heat.

2 Remove from heat and add semisweet and milk chocolate chips, stirring until smooth. Add walnuts; mix well.

3 Spread into an 8-inch square baking dish (see Tip) and chill 3 to 4 hours, or until firm. Cut into squares, and serve.

CHANGE IT UP: Before chilling the fudge, you can press some mini marshmallows and additional walnuts into the top to create Rocky Road Fudge.

TEST-KITCHEN TIP: Line your baking dish with nonstick aluminum foil for easily removing the fudge…and even easier cleanup!

Butter Pecan Fudge

Makes about 5 dozen pieces

*O*ur holiday trays and platters will be piled high with all sorts of delectable treats, but I'm betting this melt-in-your-mouth fudge will disappear first!

1/2 cup (1 stick) butter

1/2 cup heavy cream

1/2 cup granulated sugar

1/2 cup packed light brown sugar

1/8 teaspoon salt

1 cup pecan halves, toasted (see Tip)

1 teaspoon vanilla extract

2 cups confectioners' sugar

1 Coat an 8-inch square baking dish with nonstick cooking spray.

2 In a large saucepan, bring the butter, heavy cream, granulated and brown sugars, and salt to a boil over medium heat, stirring frequently. Allow to boil 5 minutes, stirring constantly.

3 Remove sugar mixture from heat and stir in pecans and vanilla. Add confectioners' sugar, and stir until smooth and well combined. Spread evenly into baking dish.

4 Freeze 25 to 30 minutes, or until firm. Cut into 1-inch squares and serve, or store in an airtight container until ready to serve.

TEST-KITCHEN TIP: To toast the pecans, heat a medium skillet over medium-low heat. When the skillet is hot, add the nuts and toast for 1 to 2 minutes, stirring frequently, until golden.

Reindeer Fudge

Makes 8 wedges

*A*ren't these decorated fudge wedges just the most adorable thing you've ever seen? Your work friends will love getting 'em from their Secret Santa, and your family will love finding 'em in their stockings.

1-1/2 cups smooth peanut butter

3/4 cup (1-1/2 sticks) butter

4-1/2 cups confectioners' sugar

1-1/2 teaspoons vanilla extract

3 tablespoons milk

1 Coat a 9-inch glass pie plate with nonstick cooking spray.

2 In a large microwave-safe bowl, combine the peanut butter and butter. Microwave at 80% power for 1 to 2 minutes.

3 Remove from microwave and add remaining ingredients; mix well then press into pie plate. Microwave at 80% power for another minute.

4 Chill in refrigerator for 1 to 2 hours, or until firm. Remove and cut into eight wedges. Wrap each piece in clear cellophane and decorate to look like a reindeer, as shown below. It's fun and really easy!

Index

Beef
Bacon-Wrapped Filets, 62
Cheeseburger Bake, 102
Dogs & Hogs, 27
Fire Station Chili, 112
Garlic-Studded Tenderloin, 65
King-Cut Prime Rib, 64
Saucy Cola Meatballs, 32
Shortcut Beef Rollups, 109

Beverages
Caramel Latte, 164
Cocoa Peppermint Frosty, 170
Hot Spiced Cider, 166
Pineapple Wassail, 166
Pomegranate Sangria, 168
S'mores Hot Cocoa, 167
White Christmas Eggnog, 167

Bread
Bacon Cheddar Rollups, 58
Candy Cane Bread Sticks, 57
Chocolate Chip Cranberry Bread, 178
Cinnamon Breakfast Wreath, 16
Cranberry Citrus Muffins, 13
Easy Mayo Rolls, 56
Festive Stromboli, 18
Kickin' Corn Bread, 55
Mediterranean Rollups, 58
Olive Focaccia, 54
Parmesan-Garlic Croutons, 44
Pumpkin Spice Bread, 60
Sour Cream & Chive Biscuits, 52
South-of-the-Border Rollups, 58
Stuffed Pizza Bites, 22
Swiss Fondue Bread, 23

Breakfast
Bananas Foster Waffles, 4
Broccoli and Cheese Quiche, 6
Cheddar 'n' Egg Pinwheels, 8
Chocolate-Stuffed French Toast, 5
Cinnamon Breakfast Wreath, 16
Country Ham & Potato Hash, 11
Overnight Strata, 7
Strawberry Breakfast Rollups, 2
Stuffed Pancake Muffins, 10
Tiramisù Pancakes, 12
Very Cherry Coffee Cake, 14

Butters, Sauces & Relishes
Chive Butter, 52
Fresh Cranberry Relish, 86
Honey Butter, 55
Horseradish Sauce, 64
Mustard Dipping Sauce, 34
Tarragon Dijon Butter, 62

Cakes, Cupcakes & Pies
Chocolate Mousse Cake, 114
Chocolate Pecan Pie, 132
North Pole Cranberry Pie, 134
Pistachio Cake, 117
Pumpkin Nut Torte, 116
Red Velvet Cake, 120
Snowman Cupcakes, 128
Very Cherry Coffee Cake, 14

Candy, Nuts & Fudge
Brickle Crunch, 176
Butter Pecan Fudge, 182
Chocolate Almond Bonbons, 174
Chocolate Walnut Fudge, 181
Cranberry Clusters, 172
Macadamia Turtles, 177
Munch and Crunch, 180
Red Cinnamon Popcorn, 175
Reindeer Fudge, 184
Sugar 'n' Spice Nuts, 172

Cheese
Cranberry-Pecan Brie, 28
Frosty the Cheese Ball, 24

Cheesecake
Cheesecake Cookie Cups, 156
No-Bake Eggnog Cheesecake, 122
Peppermint Swirl Cheesecake, 124
Ricotta Cheesecake, 123

Chicken
Buffalo Chicken Pizza, 106
Chicken Mediterranean, 67
Fancy Fast Chicken, 108
Mrs. Claus' Cranberry Chicken, 66
Wicked Raspberry Wings, 29

Chocolate
Brickle Crunch, 176
Cheesecake Cookie Cups, 156
Chocolate Almond Bonbons, 174
Chocolate Chip Cranberry Bread, 178
Chocolate Mousse Cake, 114
Chocolate Pecan Pie, 132
Chocolate Snow Drops, 152
Chocolate Snowballs, 118
Chocolate-Stuffed French Toast, 5
Chocolate Walnut Fudge, 181
Christmas Tree Brownie, 131
Church Windows, 149
Cocoa Peppermint Frosty, 170
Devilish Minty Cookies, 140
Macadamia Turtles, 177
Peanut Butter Wrap-Arounds, 162
Pretzel Squares, 150
S'mores Hot Cocoa, 167
Snow-Topped Chocolate Bars, 159

Index

Cookies & Bars
Almond-Kissed Cookies, 148
Anise Biscotti, 160
Apricot Macadamia Snowballs, 144
Butter Cutout Cookies, 142
Candy Cane Cookies, 153
Chocolate Raspberry Cake, 119
Chocolate Snow Drops, 152
Church Windows, 149
Devilish Minty Cookies, 140
Fruitcake Cookies, 151
Gingerbread People, 161
Italian Christmas Cookies, 141
Linzer Tart Cookies, 146
Mistletoe Bars, 138
Oatmeal Raisin Bars, 158
Peanut Butter Wrap-Arounds, 162
Pecan Butter Balls, 157
Pecan Tassies, 154
Pretzel Squares, 150
Snow-Topped Chocolate Bars, 159
Ten-Minute Rum Balls, 145
Thumbprint Cookies, 143

Dips
Frosty the Cheese Ball, 24
Kris Kringle Dip, 20
Layered Buffalo Dip, 21
Yuletide Buttermilk Dip, 26

Dressings
Farmer's Dressing, 50
Honey-Mustard Dressing, 50
Raspberry Vinaigrette, 46

Duck
Roasted Citrus Duck, 74

Eggs
Bacon-Stuffed Deviled Eggs, 36
Broccoli and Cheese Quiche, 6
Cheddar 'n' Egg Pinwheels, 8
Overnight Strata, 7

Fish
Fresh Catch Wellington, 78
Golden-Topped Salmon, 79

Lamb
Glazed Leg of Lamb, 73

Misc. Desserts
Chocolate Pistachio Panna Cotta, 127
Chocolate Raspberry Cake, 119
Chocolate Snowballs, 118
Christmas Tree Brownie, 131
Fresh Berry Panna Cotta, 127
Gingerbread Play Dough, 175
Holiday Panna Cotta, 127
Italian Christmas Cream, 133
Jubilee Cherry Trifle, 126
Minty Mousse, 136

Misc. Desserts, Cont.
Orange Bread Pudding, 130
Whipped Cream Dollops, 164

Pasta & Rice
Angelic Shrimp and Pasta, 82
Creamy Mushroom Risotto, 93
Ravioli Pesto Pie, 105
Red Pepper Pilaf, 87
Worth-the-Wait Lasagna, 76

Pork
Country Ham & Potato Hash, 11
Dogs & Hogs, 27
Herb-Crusted Pork Tenderloin, 72
Honey-Dijon Ham, 68
Orchard Stuffed Pork Loin, 69
Peaches Foster Glazed Ham, 70

Potatoes
Cheddar Scalloped Potatoes, 96
Country Ham & Potato Hash, 11
Creamy Smashed Potatoes, 100
Golden Potato Puffs, 33
Poinsettia Potatoes, 89
Shredded Sweet Potato Bake, 84
Spiral Baked Potatoes, 95

Salads
Black Forest Salad, 45
Greek Isles Salad, 48
Parmesan-Garlic Croutons, 44
Pear-Walnut Spinach Salad, 49
Reindeer Crunch Salad, 46
Ultimate Caesar Salad, 44

Sandwiches
Italian Sandwich Bake, 104

Shellfish
Angelic Shrimp and Pasta, 82
Bite-Sized Crab Cakes, 34
Classic Lobster Thermidor, 80
Easy Clams Casino, 30

Soups & Chili
Busy-Night Soup, 43
Creamy Mushroom Soup, 40
Escarole and Meatball Soup, 38
Fire Station Chili, 112
Harvest Pumpkin Soup, 41
Velvety Corn Soup, 42

Stuffing
Mushroom & Sausage Stuffing, 98
Popcorn Stuffing, 94

Turkey
Garden Sloppy Joes, 110
Pinot Grigio-Roasted Turkey, 75

Vegetables
Christmas Peas, 92
Jingle Bells 'n' Beans, 89
Southern Corn Casserole, 100
Spinach Soufflé, 88
Sweet Onion Tart, 90